CHURCH CHOIR DIRECTOR'S GUIDE TO SUCCESS

by
JAMES McCRAY

CHURCH CHOIR DIRECTOR'S GUIDE TO SUCCESS
by James McCray, Copyright ©1997

First Printing: October 1997

Published by
Santa Barbara Music Publishing
Post Office Box 41003
Santa Barbara, California 93140
Telephone: 805/962-5800
Fax: 805/966-7711

Library of Congress Catalog Number: 97-068790

McCray, James, 1938-
　　　Church Choir Director's Guide to Success

ISBN: 0-9648071-1-4

Copyright ©1997, Santa Barbara Music Publishing
All rights reserved

No part of this publication may be reproduced or utilized in any form or by any means, electronic or mechanical, including photocopying, recording, or by any information storage and retrieval system, without prior written permission from Santa Barbara Music Publishing, or as expressly permitted by the 1976 Copyright Act.

Dedicated to all my church choir members;
you have taught me the meaning of
committment to the church.

TABLE OF CONTENTS

PREFACE i

Chapter One
RECRUITING 1

Chapter Two
RETAINING 11

Chapter Three
REHEARSALS 29

Chapter Four
REJUVENATION 47

Chapter Five
REPERTOIRE: The Church Year 59

Chapter Six
REPERTOIRE: Variety 71

Chapter Seven
REPERTOIRE: Genres 77

Chapter Eight
RESOURCES: Funding 99

Chapter Nine
RESOURCES: Materials 109

Chapter Ten
REWARDS 119

Chapter Eleven
REMINDERS..127

Chapter Twelve
REMAINING CONCERNS
    Children's Choirs..137
    Youth Choirs..140
    Handbell Choirs...143
    Music with Additional Solo Instruments....................145
    Textual Concerns..148
    Coda..151

Appendix A
SANCTUARY CHOIR NEWSLETTER....................................155

Appendix B1
FUMC MUSIC SCHEDULE..157

Appendix B2
SANCTUARY CHOIR REPERTOIRE...................................159

Appendix C
A GOOD FRIDAY MEDITATION...161

A SELECTED BIBLIOGRAPHY...162

INDEX 165

About the Author..167

PREFACE

The church remains one of the most important active repositories for choral music. Throughout America, as well as other countries of the world, music holds a place of prominence in the weekly liturgical services of most denominations. In some, as they have been for centuries, daily services are held, and incorporated into them as one of the main features is music.

Most of our colleges and universities are not training young musicians to be church choir directors. An examination of numerous music programs available in state and private institutions not only reveals that no formal degree is offered, but in most schools, there is not even a single course which addresses this profession. Except in rare cases, students are trained to be teachers, performers, conductors, and music therapists, but not specifically church musicians. Interestingly, church musicians tend to be a combination of all of those courses of study.

There is not a scintilla of evidence that being a high school band director or a piano teacher is an appropriate correlation for those wanting to do church choir directing. Each community has many churches, usually far more than the number of schools requiring a music teacher. Yet, because schools have a more formalized certification program for hiring, it is the school degree which is emphasized. Just as elementary music teachers need skills different from those teaching high school, so it is with church choir directors compared to directors in school and community choirs. Some musical attributes are the same, but purpose and motivation contrast sharply. The proverbial axiom of the *post hoc, ergo propter hoc* fallacy (the rooster crows and the sun rises, therefore the crowing caused the sunrise) is universally accepted regarding church choir work. There is a false assumption that anyone with a music background is suited for church choirs. Sadly, that is not only the case, but is one of the prime reasons for decay in this area.

Church choir directors, generally are in part-time positions. Only very large, usually metropolitan churches, have full-time musicians on their staff. Ministers and church leaders recognize the value of music at their institutions, yet seem unwilling to seek out and hire trained people to develop a full-time comprehensive program. Naturally, part-time work and a small salary results in limited accomplishment. But, the value of music to any congregation is unlimited.

Church attendance has a serpentine path; today most churches are finding a large percentage of their flock to be in places other than the pews on Sunday morning. Christmas and Easter services swell to gigantic proportions, yet weekly attendance often is sparse. The numbers of members on a church roll may be four or five times the numbers attending on any average Sunday.

One approach to the attendance problem has been the use of a more "popular" style of music. Prescient thinkers decided that if people spent the week listening to "pop" music, then perhaps that should be the style used on Sunday mornings too. In most instances, that has not produced consistently significant increases, and at best, has been an ineffective band aid.

What is needed is the development of strong, well-educated church musicians who have a broad perspective rooted in the traditions of the church. Solid church music

Preface

programs are those where recruiting and retaining singers have been effective, and where multifaceted musical activities abound. The main choir provides musical leadership to the congregation and, in many instances, acts as glue connecting all phases of the worship service. Directors with vision, expertise in musical and social arenas, and a dedication to quality will be an important part of the growth and stability of any church.

This book is a compendium of ideas that have surfaced throughout my nearly twenty years as a church choir director. I, too, was one of those school conductors thrust into the realm of church choir work with no formal expertise. My "on the job training" was slow, often growing out of a trial process to discover what did and did not work.

My experiences as a church choir director have included both small and large churches; my first experience was in an all-male, maximum security prison where I was asked to start a new program that developed both a Protestant and a Catholic choir for the prison. Recruiting choir members in that situation was extraordinary training. Some of the techniques learned there have been useful in church environments outside the prison.

Over the years, I have discovered many different ways of accomplishing tasks; many ideas have been absorbed from a multitude of people and programs. Suggestions and ideas come from workshops, other church music programs and directors, and members of the choir. To everyone who has influenced my work habits, I offer a profound thank you. Through this book, I now am pleased to have the opportunity to share those ideas with other generations of church musicians.

This book is designed to be a resource for anyone, new or experienced, who is faced with the weekly problems of preparing a church choir for liturgical involvement. Many of the recommendations may seem obvious to those who have been church choir directors, but for those just starting out, they may be a life preserver in the sea of the unknown! It is not structured to be read from cover-to-cover, but rather as something that can be sampled. For example, users may want to start with Chapter Eleven, REMINDERS, which is a forty-item checklist of "do's and don'ts" for new and experienced directors.

The book is dedicated to all of the church choir singers I have encountered through the years. Their dedication, talent, and commitment to the church have been an inspiration which has helped me find my way through the maze. Each Sunday they reappear as a nameless face in the crowd, projecting beautiful interpretations to the congregation. They, truly, are the ones who elevate the worship and bring a deeper understanding of the Word.

Special thanks are extended to Jerome Buttera, Editor of *The Diapason* for giving me permission to extract ideas and comments from my columns on church music which have been written over the past twenty years. I am appreciative of the suggestions from the book readers. Lee Egbert (Colorado State University and Timothy Snyder (Yale Institute of Sacred Music) have both served as church choir directors, and their insights were very helpful. William Runyan (Colorado State University) and Barbara Harlow (Santa Barbara Music Publishing) provided useful, penetrating comments on the technical writing. Finally, thanks go to Colorado State University for providing me with the sabbatical leave which gave me time to think, process, write, and complete this book.

CHAPTER 1

> There let the pealing organ blow, To the full voiced choir below, In service high, and anthems clear, As may with sweetness, through mine ear Dissolve me into ecstasies, And bring all Heav'n before mine eyes.
>
> John Milton
> *Il Penseroso'*

RECRUITING

Recruiting good singers to a church choir is a primary condition of success for any conductor. In a 1986 *Journal of Church Music Survey*, recruiting was listed as "the greatest disappointment of church musicians." With the limited time available for rehearsals and the necessity for new music on a weekly basis, it is vital that the choir contain leaders with fine voices and solid reading ability. Identifying and recruiting these singers is a task that takes considerable effort and time. This is the keystone on which all other elements depend.

To merely think of the church choir in musical terms is to reduce its potential. Church choirs are comprised of people who truly *believe* what they are singing. This raises the depth of consciousness not only in them, but also in those who hear them. A choir needs a solid mixture of competent musicians and well-informed lay people who have strong commitment to the church. This combination creates a choir of unlimited capacities. The *ideal* church choir member is a rare combination of competent musician *and* dedicated congregation member.

Often, a director's personality is the connecting link that encourages interest. Volunteer church choirs are far different from professional or school ensembles. For many people, it is not the music that dominates their decision to join the choir, it is the reward of the total experience. Church choirs are built around people who want to serve the church through their individual talents; the members need to feel that their director is committed to the church and its music, and is someone who makes the rehearsals enjoyable and constructive.

The congregation needs to understand that the choir serves to enhance worship, to preserve religious musical traditions, and to illuminate THE WORD or GOSPEL. Certainly, there are many other functions of a choir, but its primary mission is to help the congregation understand texts, doctrines, and theology, and to develop an emotional response to these areas. To do this, the choir needs to be comprised of people from diverse backgrounds who bring different perspectives to the music. The following ideas have proven successful in recruiting new members who will contribute in both musical and non-musical arenas.

RECRUITING IDEAS
Recruitment Officer/Committee

The task of recruiting is a responsibility of everyone in the group, not just the director. Assign someone to be in charge of this area. Choose a respected member of the choir and the church, someone who has been around a long time and is well acquainted with the congregation. This person should receive the monthly updates of church membership enabling them to send a personal invitation from the choir to each new family/member of the church.

Form a recruiting committee to assist with all tasks relating to attracting new members; it should be comprised of people from various age groups. Often, many of the choir also participate in other groups of the church such as those for senior citizens, young couples, or singles; if they are on the lookout for new members in their special interest sphere, outreach is accomplished quickly.

Open Choir Event

Schedule a choir event such as a hymn sing or simply an open rehearsal when others can participate. This evening or post-service activity will need ample promotion, but if everyone in the choir brings just one person with them to it, the choir would be immediately doubled. Getting people to make that initial move to action is one of the primary obstacles to overcome. Often, after people experience something for the first time (swimming, flying) they find that it does not present the problem they anticipated. The old adage, *Try it, you'll like it*, definitely applies to choral singing. For many people, the main roadblock is finding a way to encourage the average singer to join a choir of excellent singers. A critical element to any recruitment program is making them feel welcome.

Music Brochure

Develop a music department brochure which covers all of the ensembles of the church. Include descriptions of each group, rehearsal times, rehearsal duration, types of music performed, usual performance times (i.e., the handbell choir always performs on third Sunday of the month), name and telephone number of director, and the name and telephone number of the person to contact for additional information. These brochures should be attractive yet succinct. Have them placed in various information areas throughout the church. In the fall, this information should be extracted to a smaller, separate brochure for all children's choirs and sent home with each child so that parents who are not regular church attendees will be made aware of choir opportunities for their children. Also, be sure to have brochures emphasize combinations of members such as wife/husband, and mother/daughter; this may encourage additional members, even though they may not be equal in musical ability.

Have these brochures included in all distributed packets of information about the church which are made available to visitors, newcomers, and those people who make inquiries searching for a new church. Often, the determining factor for people choosing a particular church stems from the minister's sermons and the music heard in the services.

Be certain that the music groups are represented in the church directory and that the music director's name and telephone number are included on all general information distributed by the church.

Networking: Within the Church

The membership secretary is an important contact, especially in a large church. Make arrangements to receive a monthly list of all new members in the church and send them a follow-up welcome to the church and personal invitation to join the choir. Include a copy of the ensemble brochures. Many churches identify visitors through various methods; obtain that list for additional contacts. It is possible that an invitation to join the choir may be the determining factor in a person's returning to or choosing a church.

Know the Sunday School teachers and youth leaders; ask them to watch for talented people who have good singing ability. They are a vital liaison for growth with each of the preadult groups. Encourage all music directors of these age

Recruiting

groups to visit each Sunday School class with invitations to attend a rehearsal and/or join the group. Have the Sunday School teacher identify friends of those singers already in your choir so that direct contact can be made with them; many young people will not join a group unless they have a friend in it, so knowing that their good Sunday School *buddy* is in the group makes it more inviting to them.

A quick, easy way to directly reach a large group of people, is to place fliers under car windshield wipers during church services. People *will* see the information and, in most cases, since this is found when they are exiting the church, will take the copy home; this is a particularly useful, fun activity for youth choirs.

Have a MUSIC BULLETIN BOARD within the church. It should be in a prominent traffic area and will require regular attention. Encourage each ensemble director to use it for announcements. Either you or someone from the choir should monitor it to be certain it has useful new information and an attractive appearance. If possible, it should be significantly changed every two weeks (i.e., new pictures, new color background) so that it continues to catch the attention of those passing by.

Identify four different times of the year as NEW MEMBERS OPPORTUNITIES (early Fall, pre-Christmas, New Year's Day, and pre-Easter). Make these times seem very special for those wanting to join the choir, although people may join at any time. Through announcements from the pulpit, the bulletin, and brochures, let it be known that this is a *great* time to join the choir. Announce that this is the time when new music is going into the folders and a period for a *fresh* start; in the cases of Christmas and Easter, each presents a time to become involved in the choir which leads to a specific purpose or conclusion. For many, singing with the choir during the Christmas season is a special treat; while some members of the congregation may feel reluctant to join a choir and make a nine-month commitment, many may share their talents for limited periods. This always has immediate benefits for everyone.

Networking: Outside the Church

A crucial factor for any church music director is knowing the community music teachers (school and private). These people can help identify vocal and instrumental musicians who may be unknown to you, yet are members of the church. Attendance at community music events is a quick way to notice personnel participating in various choirs, bands, or orchestras.

High school solo and ensemble contests are an excellent inroad into ascertaining local talent. Singers, accompanists, and instrumentalists can be quickly identified through these events; usually, those participating in the contests are the ones who have the most interest in music, and therefore are the ones most likely to want to join a group. This is particularly useful in seeking instrumentalists to play in a church orchestra or as an obbligato part on an anthem. Hearing them play a solo quickly categorizes their level of ability; in some cases, these solos may be appropriate for use within a service as special music which immediately draws the performer into the program through a piece of music already perfected.

Gimmick Announcements

In addition to the more formal announcements given by the minister, the director, or someone from the choir, congregations greatly enjoy unique approaches to distribution of information. Using puppets or skits to spread the word is a fun way to attract attention to the message. One of the most effective mini-skits can be patterned after Bill Cosby's famous *Noah's Conversation with God* (deep offstage voice).

Recruiting

A delightful way of reaching people is to create a brief, two-minute script for presentation during the community time before the service begins. Use music and/or singing in the choir as the vehicle and feature well-known church personalities.

Puppets work very well for children's interest; prerecord a conversation on cassette tape and have the puppeteer hide the tape on her/his body or in the puppet. A very effective conversation can take place that will capture the focus of all children (and adults); record the puppet's words, and then by stopping the tape during the conversation, allow time for the puppeteer to speak creating a conversation. Some use the process of blank space on the tape, but that is less effective because audience reactions such as laughter may interrupt the flow of the conversation.

Church Survey

An all-church survey done every few years is a beneficial method of identifying musicians. For new directors this is especially valuable. The survey should be short and ask only those questions that would be of use to the director. In addition to basics such as name, address and phone number, a survey should seek information about musical areas such as singing and instrumental experience, instruments played, and interest in future involvement.

This type of survey could be a part of a larger all-church survey seeking other types of content, or simply be a brief music survey. As an insert in the weekly bulletin, it can be deposited in the collection plate during a Sunday service. Only those who have an initial interest will likely return the survey; the others often refuse to be identified for fear of being contacted.

The most difficult next step is that of ascertaining the level of musicianship of the instrumentalist who has responded to the survey. Discussions with performers do not always result in a true level since they may exaggerate or underestimate their ability. If possible, for the initial evaluation find an opportunity for the instrumentalist to play with the group on something where they are not the only person on that part. This will avoid embarrassing situations for all concerned. Playing an exposed obbligato solo or being the only cello in a small accompanying string ensemble requires a definite ability, and a full assessment before rehearsing with the choir is strongly recommended. It is better to move instrumentalists from group performance into solo roles rather than the reverse.

Video Compilation

Make a video which involves all phases of the music program. This compilation does not need to feature complete performances of groups or compositions, but rather should have a comprehensive spirit which gives the impression of something for everyone. Vary the types of music included so that there are examples of serious Latin motets and rhythmic spirituals. Include examples where the congregation is singing with the choir as well as music that is accompanied by more than just organ.

The tape should have a broad appeal. Use excerpts from the Christmas and Easter services, special programs; include soloists, processionals, and other types of visual effects. It is important that in addition to the musical performances, scenes be included of informal fun events. With minimal effort these events could have the music of the choir dubbed over them as in a documentary film.

Be very certain that the sound on the tape has a high quality. The video should reveal a very positive impression that being involved in the church music program is fun, communicative, and genuine to individual and group worship environments.

Recruiting

This tape could be shown during social hours after church services, at various group meetings within the church, and on other special occasions such as during information sessions for new members of the church. The tape should be kept to about twenty minutes maximum duration so that it could fit into a variety of situations. Have several copies of the tape. The work put into the development of the tape will pay off for many years to come.

Provide Music for Church Classes/Groups

Let the various Sunday School classes and groups (clubs) within the church know that you are interested in providing music for them. Although this probably would not involve the large choir, owing to time commitments, it would be possible to organize a group of solos or duets for these occasions. This functions particularly well in those churches where the choir has a large number of retired people available during the day. The director could organize a list of singers and instrumentalists interested in providing music and then serve as a clearinghouse for scheduling. Or, this could be handled by a separate person or committee within the choir; again, a retired person would be most useful. This kind of assistance to other divisions in the church is valuable to them; it will be remembered at those times when the music program needs new robes, additional handbells, or more music.

These types of performances could be offered outside of the home church. Community activities are always seeking talented performers; this outreach beyond the church has many benefits for recruitment for the music program and the entire church.

Welcome Wagon

Have someone in the choir serve as the official welcomer for the choir, in much the same way that many communities have a welcome wagon person who visits the new family bringing information about the community. This person could be in charge of sizing new members for a robe, assigning them a box (slot) for music storage, getting them a new folder, introducing them to other choir members, and answering any questions they might have about choir procedures. It is best to have one coordinator for this, and to have one person from each section of the choir act as the section host. The coordinator would introduce the new member to the host who would, in turn, introduce them to others in the section and sit with them during the rehearsal. This will make new members immediately comfortable within the choir. Also, the personal warmth of the choir will be felt if you, as director, take new members for coffee after their first rehearsal.

New Person Ceremony

There should be some brief activity during the new members' first rehearsal which introduces them to the choir. This mini-ritual could include such things as giving a brief biographical sketch of them or presenting them with their choir robes and an official choir coffee cup. These gestures will serve to make them feel extra welcome.

Recruiting new choir members is a never-ending part of the responsibility for the music director. Even though Shakespeare in *The Winter's Tale* said, "The silence often of pure innocence persuades when speaking fails," directors and choir members should constantly recruit additional singers in all ways possible.

CHAPTER 2

At one end of the spectrum there is the kind of communication which one may compare with the passing from hand to hand of an object—a parcel, a book, a piece of paper, while at the other end there is a communication which is much more like the throwing of a ball. In the former case, the recipient simply takes it; in the latter, he catches it—or drops it. In the second, but not in the first, there is an element of risk, (he may drop it) and an element of personal effort and satisfaction (if he catches it). In the first case, there is nothing personal in the transaction; in the other, there is a personal factor which may easily amount to a factor of change: something happens to the person who catches the ball.

Erik Routley
The Divine Formula

RETAINING

It has been said that *getting money is not difficult, keeping it is the hard part*. So it is with church choir members. A typical church choir membership is a mixture of those who are regulars, and have been for years, contrasted with those who are as passengers on a bus entering and exiting with great freedom. The challenge is to co-mingle them so that consistency and continuity are achieved.

Some directors have specific rules regarding involvement. For example, to miss the mid-week rehearsal means that the singer can not perform on the next Sunday. This severe regimentation seems to lose sight of the purpose of the choir. Is quality seriously reduced by permitting someone to sing who missed the final rehearsal? I doubt it. If the choir has been rehearsing the music for several weeks so that the singer has some knowledge of it, she or he will contribute to the service, which is precisely the task of choir members. It is not reasonable to expect a volunteer choir, which rehearses every week for at least nine months, to have perfect attendance. There will be conflicts that must take precedence over the volunteer church choir. One characteristic of a successful church director is flexibility, and where weekly involvement of the church choir singer is concerned, that is extremely consequential.

A church program, in order to succeed, needs considerable breadth so there is appeal to a wide variety of tastes. Those programs which become mechanical and predictable soon fade. With each year and, in fact, each month, there must be new phases to the rehearsals and the music, to sustain interest.

In addition to feeling welcome and valued, the choir members have to be challenged and rewarded. They need to express individual spiritual growth and know that what they are doing is respected and exigent. In the midst of all this, there is also the social element. A vital criteria to any volunteer group is the fun element; singers must enjoy the rehearsals and the camaraderie with those of similar interests. The director must be cognizant of these needs and nurture them. Then, retaining members and building a larger more active program will result, and in turn, recruiting becomes easier because people want to be a part of something meaningful and successful. *Success breeds success.*

Retaining

Effective church choir directors arm themselves with new and expanding ideas for making the choir feel (and be) successful. They must establish distinct and dissimilar reasons for people to show up each week. The lack of commitment is one of the twentieth-century's ills. Enduring relationships are less frequent than in the past, so keeping a reservoir of good musicians who make quality, weekly musical contributions to the worship service is something that requires constant nourishing.

RETAINING CHOIR MEMBERS
Names

Be certain you know all of your choir members by name; for small choirs that is not a problem, but in larger choirs with numerous transient members that sometimes is difficult. Nametags, while useful at the beginning of the year, quickly lose their effectiveness. Singers feel it is unnecessary to put them on each week and on Sundays they cannot be worn on their robes. Use them for one or two weeks and then abandon them.

It is easy to feature each section of the choir at one rehearsal One method, which blends names and social concerns, is to have one section of the choir responsible for post-rehearsal refreshments. Each member of that choir section brings some small refreshment such as juice and cookies. That, then, affords the director an opportunity to announce that,

> Tonight's rehearsal and post-rehearsal social is brought to us by The Alto Section. Would they please stand and introduce themselves so that we can properly thank them.

Doing that four weeks in row to cover all sections goes a long way in creating an *esprit de corps* among the members and also helps everyone learn many of the names of the group.

Personal Achievements

Announce and use the music bulletin board to celebrate the achievements of those in the choir. Through newspaper clippings and other sources of information, herald the good news. Community and school activities often go unnoticed; sharing the success of individuals with the choir is a great morale booster. It makes everyone glad they are there. We all need that "pat on the back;" volunteer choir members *deserve* the attention.

Personal Notes

In addition to the group announcements, a director should send personal notes to choir members. These can pertain to their achievements, be a thank you note for doing some chore for the music area, or simply be a note of appreciation for other, less recognized circumstances. How refreshing it is to receive a note which gives thanks for being very attentive in the rehearsal or for showing musical leadership during the repeated practicing of a difficult passage. Throughout the course of a year, try to send a personal note of gratitude to everyone in the choir. Their response to you for taking the time to do so will be overwhelming.

Choir Newletter

Develop a choir newsletter which has two parts to it. One part is the distribution of functional information such as performance schedules, extra rehearsals, repertoire, and items of a perfunctory nature. The other part should be of a more personal essence. Provide information about choir members, about special comments passed along to you from members of the congregation, about liturgical observations relating to the music they will be performing, perhaps a poem or a joke or a poignant quote, and always end with

Retaining

positive comments about the singers' contributions to the worship services (See Appendix A).

Develop a personal logo for the choir and use it on all of their publications. Try to have a newsletter once a month so that everyone is aware of the past and future activities of the group. This group connection is very helpful in keeping people informed, especially those who miss a rehearsal. Spoken announcements are only useful for those in attendance; directors need to be certain they are reaching every singer, including those *part-timers* who only sing twice a month.

Missed You Cards

Send cards to choir members for special occasions such as *happy birthday*, *get well*, and especially *missed you*. The missed you card calls to their attention that they were missed from a rehearsal which strongly, yet subtly, encourages them to be there next week. Even though you may use cards with prepared messages, it is very important that you include a personal, hand written greeting as well.

Make time for hospital visits to choir members. Usually, the minister or main office will have a record of all church people who are in the hospital; a visit from their director will be greatly appreciated. Cards, notes, visits, and other similar expressions remind the choir that not only are they important, but that you are a caring, concerned person who is truly interested in more than just their voice!

Singer of the Month

An excellent way of spotlighting members of the choir is to designate a singer of the month. This could be a feature in each monthly newsletter. Include the singer's interests, some reason (musical or non-musical) why he or she was selected that month, a quote from or about the person which relates to the choir or music, and, if possible, a picture. In addition, to the newsletter, put this information on the all-church music bulletin board. Highlighting individuals in the choir is an easy, effective method of building morale and group dynamics.

Choir Retreat

An ideal way to bring a choir together is to have an annual retreat filled with rehearsals and social events. Hold the retreat at summer's end as a kickoff for the new season to establish an immediate rapport with the group, and to provide ample opportunities for the choir to learn new repertoire. Retreats take various formats, some with overnight stays, some as an all-day short travel event, and some merely as an extended occasion in the local church. All feature a mixture of rehearsals, games, and eating; many include a worship service as part of the retreat. This adds a personal dimension to the choir's primary function.

Careful pre-planning is needed for these events. Problems of a small turnout, poor travel arrangements and high basic costs, poor weather forcing all indoor activities, and not enough fun group adventures can begin the year with negative consequences. Yet, with adequate organization and an agreeable time for the retreat, it can hasten group cohesion and quickly establish a feeling of unity.

Schedules

It is imperative to provide the choirs and various ensembles with detailed schedules. The director must structure all of the music events for the church. Small churches may have only one service each week; larger churches will have several, and all need some type of music. Other musical events, concerts, special services, additional rehearsals, should also be carefully planned and announced.

Retaining

Two types of schedules are suggested (See Appendix B). The first one is a general weekly schedule which extends from August to September and/or January through May. This schedule merely chronicles the services and additional performances so that the musicians can mark their calendars early. The other schedule, a monthly calendar, includes all anthems and service music for the month. These calendars should be distributed about two weeks prior to that month; the general calendar is distributed on the first rehearsal at the start of the new season.

Careful organization by the director does not insure that people will be there, but it does increase the possibility for solid attendance. Often people can avoid conflicts with early notification.

Participation in Liturgy

The choir will have a more liturgical function if they are involved in several aspects of the service. To only prepare an anthem and sing it each week tends to put them in the classification of entertainers; however, singing other types of music such as an introit, a prayer response, or a benediction, places them in a different role. They actively are collegial liturgists. Having beautiful singing throughout the service gives it an elevation of dignity and continues to keep the congregation and choir emotionally involved.

Planning for and rehearsing additional music for these service functions does require additional time, but it can be accomplished with minimal effort. Singing a simple hymn refrain is an easy, fast method of creating purposeful service music. Amens, anthem fragments, and simple unison hymn melodies can be used throughout the service. These short excerpts may be used several times throughout the year. The development of a ceremonial repertoire for liturgy is not as time consuming as it may seem.

Spacial Singing

The choir should sing from places other than the traditional choir loft. The use of processionals is an effective, dramatic way to begin a service; however, it is recommended that this be done occasionally rather than weekly. Place the choir in a balcony for an unaccompanied introit or anthem to add power to the music and give a new perspective to the sound. Singing from other places within a sanctuary adds a fresh spirit to the performance. Arrange the choir in separate or mixed sections in various places of sanctuary to sing canonically to give the music an intoxicating sense of wonder. Antiphonal music which is performed effectively always thrills a congregation and brings to the music a greater sense of present and past, foreground and echo.

Choir Exchange for Worship Services

A choir exchange with another church is a delightful way of sustaining interest. By exchanging with another denomination, an ecumenical spirit can be fostered. Exchanges take two basic forms:

  a. choirs change churches on the same day (rather perfunctory);
  b. host choirs remain at their churches to assist the visiting choir with details (preferred).

The latter takes two separate Sundays and is more social and, for first time exchanges, is best. However, if groups did exchanges each year, it would be easy to simply do it on the same day because everyone would have experience with the new church and better understand their liturgy process.

There are many advantages to this kind of activity. Congregations and ministers usually enjoy having a visiting choir. Choir members have an opportunity to hear a different choir and/or sing in a new environment. And, in the case of different denominations, new perspectives on liturgy are seen. This is valuable for singers and the director.

The choice of exchanges should be carefully reviewed. For best results, the two choirs should be at about the same performance level. Exchanges involving a large, musically advanced choir paired with one that is smaller and less polished, often result in problems for directors for obvious reasons. The purpose of exchanges should not be seen as competitive, but rather as spiritual and social. If the director sets the tone of the exchange as an opportunity for sharing and learning from one another, problems will not result.

Special Worship Services

Church choirs, unlike school or community choirs, cover more repertoire. A school choir will learn a few works for each concert, and, perhaps, only present four concerts a year. Church choirs need to be prepared to sing anywhere from thirty to forty times a year just for services. That means that they have the chance to explore more repertoire. The director should be certain to use diverse types of music (see repertoire chapter), and also find ways of using some new formats in the weekly service These kinds of changes need the cooperation and suggestions of the minister. Although it should not be done too often, perhaps twice a year, designing a worship service around such conditions as new hymns, liturgical dance, a special theme or person (Biblical heroes), a style (black spirituals, early American services) or an idea (love, healing, commitment) will give the congregation new insights. One that is of particular interest to ministers is the teachings of Jesus. Some of these topics such as Biblical heroes, commitment, or the sayings of Jesus, would be useful as a month-long study for worship services. These kinds of topics could be used in ancillary church activities which go beyond a worship service, such as extended Lenten studies.

Consider using the basic idea of the traditional Christmas Service, *Lessons and Carols*, but pattern it after some other season or theme. (See Appendix C). Times such as Ash Wednesday or Maundy Thursday are easily adapted. This kind of service has a Scripture reading followed by a musical reflection of that text. By alternating congregational hymn singing with choir performances, everyone stays involved throughout. A short homily (sermon) could still be included, keeping the service anchored.

A service of Psalms and Psalm interpretation is a cheerful type of alternate worship. Here, the choir prepares a series of anthems on Psalm texts. After they are sung, the minister then gives brief interpretative comments and background about the Psalm. Many hymns are based on Psalms. With careful planning, it would be possible to arrange a format for each Psalm:

    a. choir sings Psalm

    b. minister discusses Psalm

    c. congregation sings hymn based on Psalm.

There are many kinds of topic areas which could be explored.

Church Festivals

There are three ways of having the choir participate in special performances. A simple way is to work directly with another local church in the preparation of a major work. For example, a joint production of Faure's *Requiem* for a Good Friday performance will expand the quantity and quality of the choir. The two churches, then, could share expenses for the orchestra, programs, and publicity. This should be planned as a two-year event so that each director and each church could serve as host. The second year the groups could do a different requiem such as one by Rutter or Mozart. Choirs would work independently on the movements and, in fact, use some of the music in Lenten worship services leading up to the complete work. Then, two combined rehearsals with the orchestra would bring the music into a polished state.

Another type of festival is one which involves many churches in a one-day rehearsal and concert arrangement. In these cases, the entire choir usually is not involved—it is open to those interested. Here, a guest conductor/clinician might be used. Repertoire often consists of a variety of anthems so that each church could then use them in their own services after the festival. In these events, the performance is probably less significant than the rehearsals. A guest conductor who brings new ideas for tone development, rehearsal techniques, and other choral matters, is quite valuable for both the conductor and the choir.

The third type of festival features international travel. Festivals in England with church choir people from all over the world have become exciting, worthwhile events. These combined choirs are quite large and generally feature a famous conductor and professional orchestra performing an extended major work such as the *Requiem* of Verdi or Brahms. International festivals include the possibility for the church choir to tour on its own after the conclusion of the festival; some offer the prospect for interested choirs to do a performance tour giving concerts at churches. This kind of motivational activity requires considerable preparatory work. It will become something that brings the group into a firm family relationship and will become a cherished memory for all.

Choir Dedication Sunday

At the beginning of each new choir year, schedule a special dedication as part of the first Sunday services in which they sing. This not only gives the choir recognition for the work they are about to do, but also instills a sense of commitment. Often, the first Sunday the choir sings in the fall is also *rally Sunday* for the entire church. This is the day when Sunday School begins for students at their new level and other latent church activities resume.

The service could include such hymns as *Take My Life and Let It Be, Come, Christians, Join To Sing,* or *Oh Jesus, I Have Promised.* A scripture that is appropriate is Colossians 3:15-17 which says,

> The peace that Christ gives is to guide you in the decisions you make; for it is to this peace that God has called you together in the one body. And be thankful. Christ's message in all its richness must live in your hearts. Teach and instruct one another with all wisdom. Sing psalms, hymns, and sacred songs; sing to God with thanksgiving in your hearts. Everything you do or say, then should be in the name of Lord Jesus, as you give thanks through him to God the Father.

That scripture could be read by the minister after which this Sanctuary Choir Creed would be recited by the choir:

> We, the Sanctuary Choir of _____ in the city of _____, do dedicate ourselves this ____day of September, _____, to the coming term of Christian service to serve our God, our church, and each other. Our purpose is to bring glory to God; our medium is the God-given gift of music. We are only able to make this pledge by the power that God gives us, by His Son, through the work of the Holy Spirit. It is our responsibility, therefore, to value this pledge with honor and duty.

An appropriate anthem for this type of service is Charles Callahan's *A Musician's Prayer* for SATB/organ (Randall M. Egan Co.). It is easy, brief, and has a scintillating text by

Retaining

William Austin that suitably speaks to the work and commitment of the volunteer choir. Another suitable text, either spoken or sung, is St. Francis of Assisi's, *Lord Make Me an Instrument*.

The choir could stand at the altar or in their normal places when they give their pledge. The creed should be duplicated and posted in the choir room, and for an even stronger dramatic impact, ask each choir member to sign the pledge.

This kind of ceremony makes a lasting impression on the singers. Since it occurs as part of the worship service in front of the entire church, it underscores their important contribution to the life of the church. Clearly, the new year begins on a very uplifting feeling. Following the service there should be a social of some kind; highly recommended is a covered dish picnic which helps acquaint people and brings their first Sunday of singing to a happy, communal close.

Music of the Church Series

Part of our role as church musicians is to preserve the musical heritage of the church. Set up a concert series for your church which features both guest and local church performers. Try to balance it with instrumental and vocal music. This series could be for evenings or Sunday afternoons. With careful planning, it can be a fund raiser, although a more significant aspiration is to provide quality, meaningful music for the church.

Concerts by the church organist or a guest organist should be included in the series. An all-church ensemble concert that features the children's choirs, handbell groups, and all adult choirs, will certainly generate a huge, enthusiastic audience. There could be a concert which features many of the church's vocal soloists. Or, as mentioned earlier, there could be a festival concert featuring a major work or a joint concert with another church choir. The shape of the series will evolve over the years as the audience preferences become clear. It is recommended that each year, the series feature at least one professional name soloist or group. This will be helpful in terms of selling season tickets since it insures the buyer a ticket for that special guest. Early scheduling and innovative publicity are essential characteristics of a successful series. Keep in mind that some seed money will be needed at first, but eventually these series survive on their own.

Church Staff Participation

As a special treat, have the entire church staff of ministers, custodians, and secretaries sing with the choir during a service. That adds a bold yet mirthful disposition to any service. For the choir, having these people sing with them is a time of joy. Furthermore, for the staff, spending some brief time in an intense or rollicking rehearsal is a valuable education.

Implementation of this suggestion will require premeditated thought to find the best way of encouraging the staff to attend a rehearsal and sing with the choir in a service. However, once they do it, they usually find that it is great fun, and it could become an annual event.

Form Sub-Groups

Every choir has eager singers for whom one rehearsal a week is not enough. Form smaller ensembles from within the main choir; they can serve the church in numerous capacities. A select chamber choir or a quartet (gospel or straight) can add a new dimension to any program. These groups can rehearse before or after the regular weekly rehearsal and may be used within the service to give the regular choir a week off, particularly after a heavy period of music making, such as Holy Week. They also may assist with special music programs for other church events.

Our church has three services each Sunday morning, with the first one in a smaller chapel. In the past, the 8:00 A.M. chapel service always had a soloist for the anthem/offertory slots. Since we formed a chamber choir, their responsibility has been to sing one chapel service a month; the response has been outstanding. The chapel is small enough that the chamber choir can be placed in a circle around the outer walls to surround the congregation so when they sing, the sound envelopes the listener. The chamber church choir only has about sixteen voices which lends itself to singing unaccompanied Renaissance motets and gentle accompanied anthems. By staying an extra twenty minutes twice a month, this chamber choir of enthusiastic singers not only provides a desperately needed function, but they also encounter a different kind of literature from the larger choir. Singing in a chamber choir where there are only a few voices on each part gives the performer an extra thrust of confidence; skills rapidly improve in this environment.

Create An All-Church Recording

A compact disc of the choir and/or various ensembles within the church can be a substantial fund raiser as well as a means of promoting the choir. To assist with sales, the CD probably should feature favorite congregational and choir anthems. Making a recording today is a reasonably simple process. Recording companies can bring sensitive microphones and tape recorders to the church, and can modify the final tape so that your choir sounds even better than usual!

Include several groups on the CD and the audience factor increases and more sales occur. Using different groups with diverse directors also reduces the main director's responsibility. Be sure to include an organ solo and the handbell choir; this lessens the rehearsal factor for the choir and its director.

Explain Musical Symbolism

Choir members (and the congregation) are fascinated with symbolic underpinning in all forms of art. Bach, for example, is full of symbolism in his scores. Explaining various elements of symbols and representations in the score greatly enhances the choir's understanding and ultimately their performance of the music. For example, Bach's method of representing sin is to write a curvy, musical line in the form of a snake and place it in the pedals or lower strings; for Bach, sin was traced back to the Garden of Eden and the temptation of the snake with Adam and Eve. Seeing that realized in the score springs the music to life for the performers. His numerology interests are well documented and provide a seductive ambiance to any rehearsal.

Art, visual or aural, is filled with all kinds of hidden elements which, in one way or another, guided the creator into the process. While a picture or music can be appreciated and enjoyed without knowing those intimate details, they do greatly enrich the artistic encounters. Directors are urged to research artistic symbolism and to include it as a motivating technique in their rehearsals (See bibliography of useful resources, Chapter Nine).

Guest Conductors and Composers

Work with other conductors and/or composers to bring refreshing depth to a choir. Weak conductors often fear bringing someone in to work with their choirs because their own work will be seen as inferior Everyone has strengths and weaknesses in terms of musical technique; people recognize that and, for the most part, accept it. To invite another conductor to work with your choir WILL have positive compensation. Conductor exchanges give everyone encouragement; they are an easy, inexpensive way of achieving variety within churches. These exchanges could result in a service involvement, but that is not necessary. A simple rehearsal exchange can accomplish significant enthusiasm within a choir.

If the composer or arranger of one of the choir's pieces lives near, invite the person to rehearse and/or listen to their composition to offer comments; this is always stimulating to those performing. (See chapter three for additional details involving composers and commissioning new works.) Usually these creative artists are happy to see that their music is being purchased and used; however, a small honorarium still is recommended when inviting them for an informal rehearsal.

Historian

Keep a yearly scrapbook for the music department's achievements to provide a reliable chronicle of their activities. Assign someone to be the official historian to collect programs, pictures, and other memorabilia. Be certain to include separate divisions for each musical group in the church. This scrapbook can be presented to the choir at their first fall rehearsal; reviewing the past year's accomplishments during a social hour after that first rehearsal will be a sturdy motivator for the new year and a reminder of the fun and success of the previous year. For new personnel, it is a candid, enticing orientation; for the church, it is an engaging collection of the past. At special all-church events such as a bazaars or ice cream socials, have these scrapbooks on a table for people to examine; new singers and/or handbell ringers may be enticed into the music department.

Other Non-traditional Groups

Many churches form non-traditional groups whose members do not participate in the main choir. In addition to the more common children's and youth choirs, consider having a choir comprised of people over seventy years of age. They could meet and prepare occasional music (i.e., one anthem every few months which could be used in a service). Pop music ensembles and theatre groups also can add variety to the total church program Having more outlets for diverse musical interests helps sustain congregational interest, draws in outside performers who eventually may join the choir, and provides opportunities of relief from the burden of the weekly routines.

As with recruiting, retaining singers in a church choir requires an ever-present attention. People need to feel appreciated and to be musically challenged in order to sustain interest. Even Publilius Syrus in the first century realized that when he pronounced, *"It is more easy to get a favor from Fortune than to keep it."*

CHAPTER 3

> We are steersmen, not oarsmen.
>
> Franz Liszt
> *Letter on Conducting*

REHEARSALS

Rehearsals must be a time of intensified joy. They need to be a balance of concentrated work and unbridled fun.

Singers especially need physical relaxation as a part of the rehearsal since their instrument is their body. To produce good tone and a beautiful sound, a lack of excessive tension is required. This is not to suggest poor posture or a relaxed focus, but rather an attitude. Choirs function differently than bands/orchestras, particularly in rehearsals. They require the same kind of discipline, yet egos need to be massaged more, particularly in a volunteer group. Furthermore, instrumental ensembles usually rehearse less than choirs in preparation for a performance; sustaining the development of a choral composition over a longer period of time demands a thoughtful course of action. Typically, church choirs will have many singers whose reading level is weak, so that "punching notes" may be common in the early stages of learning a work. In instrumental groups more autonomy is exhibited and drill pertains to refining intonation and phrasing rather than simply producing the musical line.

The conductor's rehearsal technique in making mundane learning interesting often is the determining factor in retaining singers and producing consistently cogent performances. Church choir rehearsals generally are once a week and last from sixty to ninety minutes. Concerts, major services such as Easter or Christmas, and other special times will require extended rehearsals. Preparing a choir for a weekly performance of one or two anthem-length compositions and additional incidental service music dictates judicious preparation and efficiency. As Ray Robinson points out in *The Choral Experience*, "Planning the rehearsal is one of the most important responsibilities of the conductor, yet it is probably also one of the most neglected."

The life of a church anthem goes through four stages

Stage one, three weeks before use
Sight read through the entire setting to introduce it to the choir; if in a foreign language, sing once in English.

Stage two, two weeks before use
Read through the easiest and most enjoyable sections (refrains, codas, etc.) spending a few minutes on cleaning up errors and establishing the mood; present background material on the composer and basic musical style.

Stage three, one week before use
Rehearse the remaining sections with the same process used in the preceding week, but spend more time on the music; read through the entire work to give the choir a sense of the moods, tempo changes; present in-depth observations on the textual message.

Stage four, final rehearsal
Rehearse the seams between the sections and fine tune the remaining music problems; sing through entire work at least twice and focus on expression.

Conductors may modify this outline to fit their own choirs; however, a basic structure similar to this should be a natural part of the rehearsal process. Much depends on the sight-reading ability of the choir, and their basic musicianship. The decisive implication, though, is that for church choirs with revolving volunteers who do not attend every rehearsal, early introduction and steady repetitions which concentrate on dissimilar areas within the music will deliver the work on time for the entire group. This kind of minimal spacing attends to detail improvement without resulting in the singers' loss of interest because of repetitive boredom.

Conductors must be meticulous in their planning for each rehearsal. A fundamental outline as a guide for preparation should be followed, and contain these elements:

- sequence the order for music to be rehearsed
- warm-ups (physical and vocal)
- pace of the rehearsal (build in vocal rest)
- absolute goals for accomplishment
- nonmusical elements (prayer, joke, announcements, etc.,)
- energize the ending/conclusion of the rehearsal

Directors may modify this outline into more explicit detail. To be consistently successful, an intricate blueprint for each rehearsal should be plotted. Some tips which might be overlooked follow.

Prayer Opening/Closing

Begin and/or end your rehearsals with a prayer and perhaps a brief message which, in some way, relates to sacred music. A poem, Psalm, or simple scriptural comment which has a musical relationship will set the mood for the evening. Many choir members have a true stewardship inclination and would be thrilled to be given the task of presenting an opening or closing prayer. These spiritual concerns only take two or three minutes, and they certainly help define the difference in this choir's purpose from those in the schools and community. If the prime mission is serving the liturgy on Sunday, then staying connected in mid-week seems highly appropriate.

Rehearsal Structure

Rehearsal preparation begins with studying the score. Design a navigation path that will clarify the text and music, anticipate and ultimately solve technical problems, and determine interpretation. Musicians are trained to do this as a natural part of the conducting experience. What is often overlooked, however, is the need to find that equilibrium between consistent rehearsal patterns and changing patterns.

Consistent procedures may include the following for a sixty minute rehearsal:

- opening prayer
- vocal warm-ups
- sight reading new anthems
- detailed work on future anthems
  (see suggested four-week outline above)
- announcements (allows vocal rest)
- perfect all incidental service music
  (introits, prayer responses, etc.)
- perfect anthems for coming Sunday
- closing prayer/comments

There are two schools of thought on rehearsals. One is that the most important work is done at the beginning while everyone is fresh, and the other is that the intense work is in the last half of the rehearsal when everyone is vocally prepared. With volunteer church groups having little vocal background, the latter seems to work best. Latecomers still have time to do some light singing before the more trenchant work on the Sunday repertoire where full-voice singing is needed. The rehearsal builds toward music to be performed so that the rehearsal ends with those compositions as a lasting reminder for Sunday.

Changing Rehearsal Elements

Beyond the consistent rehearsal structure, a director should develop the habit of preparing new elements to enrich the weekly rehearsal. This dedication of planning will make each rehearsal unique and interesting to the choir. Areas to consider are:

- a new warm-up
- a new rehearsal technique
- a new piece of instruction; make certain that they are aware a learning process is taking place; church/music history is a prime example
- something humorous
- something unusual in the score or nonmusical
- something that features a member of the choir

To include two or three of these categories into each rehearsal will sustain attention and breathe life into each week's practice time. Balancing these items with the consistent pattern of the schedule gives rehearsals stability and innovation, the desired combination.

Pre-rehearsal Details

An experienced director will attend to other mundane details that will help create a rewarding rehearsal. For example, have music in the folders, have enough copies with extras for unexpected singers, have rehearsal/service repertoire on the blackboard to encourage the choir to organize their individual folders, and have needed equipment ready for use (piano, tape recorder.) This will save valuable time for everyone.

Energizing the Rehearsal

Mindful directors will use ways of keeping everyone alert. Standing and sitting throughout the rehearsal will encourage physical attention. Change the seating (standing) arrangement during a rehearsal to give a new sound and energy. For example, move from sections into a *shotgun* (random) formation to add vigor to the choir. People enjoy sitting by someone new; hearing a different part directly in one's ear tends to improve tone and/or intonation.

Several useful rehearsal techniques which add a fresh dimension to a rehearsal are:

- Change the tempo on a work that is known (speeding or slowing the tempo dramatically presents a new perspective.)
- Reverse the dynamics on a work that is known.
- Have the choir sing silently but express the music vividly with their face.
- Rehearse accompanied passages unaccompanied.
- Sing in a circle or in some other place in the sanctuary.
- In the middle of a rehearsal have the choir hum or sing a simple, unison tune such as Amazing Grace; have them close their eyes and concentrate on the sound of the words; this is especially useful to relieve tension.

Singing Styles

Early each year, the choir needs to develop the understanding of the four basic singing styles. These styles dominate most choral music; the clear differentiations within an anthem will immediately raise the quality level of the performance. The four basic styles to be mastered are:

Rehearsals

<u>Legato</u>: very smooth, connected lines indicated by a slur

<u>Portato</u>: slightly detached articulations on syllables/words indicated by ⊙

<u>Staccato</u>: short, crisp, light notes with space between each syllable indicated by a dot •

<u>Marcato</u>: heavy, accented attacks on a note indicated by V

In teaching these articulations, one useful approach is to remind the choir that each note, no matter how long it is sung, is divided into three parts—effective singing gives attention to each area. The front part concerns attack, the back part release, and the middle is the color of the sound. For clarity, use a visual example on a chalk board.

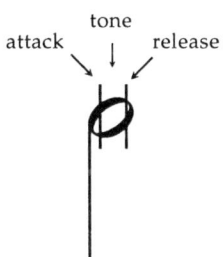

Further define the basic styles: portato is more concerned with the release; marcato is an attack articulation. Establish these differences early in the year and save enormous rehearsal time because you then only have to use one word (i.e., legato) to shape the choir's lines.

Intonation Problems

In a non-select volunteer choir, intonation is certain to be a common problem. Directors can minimize, but probably not totally eliminate, pitch discrepancies. To meet once a week with a shifting personnel common to church choirs, achieving absolute, consistent intonation perfection may never occur; however, directors need to be aware of what causes singers to sing under pitch, and to use the rehearsal as a time to solve as many of the causes as is possible. The most widespread reasons are:

- breath control, air flow, wasted breath, poor posture
- lack of forward resonance
- physical and mental fatigue/no alertness
- vocal range problems
- chest tone carried into upper register
- too many heavier timbered voices
- too much heat in the room
- acoustics lack of resonance in the room
- repeated notes and difficult pitches in different voice ranges
- poor tongue placement, rigid jaw and throaty quality

A very strong section leader with good intonation usually will greatly reduce serious pitch problems as the weaker singers migrate to that sound/pitch. The tolerance level of the conductor is an important factor. Those directors who "crave" the in-tune chord and teach singers to listen carefully ultimately will develop improvement. Proper singing habits and techniques will be the "gain" members receive from being in the group.

Problem Intervals and Melodic Considerations

Certain intervals have a larger capacity for creating intonation dilemmas than others. A director may anticipate pitch complications by identifying those intervals before the rehearsal and using the warm-ups as a time to isolate and stabilize them; then, move from the warm-up examples directly to the score where these intervals occur, and improvement will be immediate. The intervals and melodic notes which consistently drag down the pitch of most choirs are:

- the fourth and fifth degrees of the minor scale
- the third, sixth, and seventh steps in chords

- the augmented step
- leading tones, especially in inner parts
- the seventh step, especially in modulation
- descending scale steps (usually too large)
- melodies that descend and suddenly turn upward
- three or more notes sung in a downward line

Keys play a role in intonation. Generally F and C provide the most difficulty. Roger Wagner, one of America's significant choral pioneers and conductors, transposed music away from these pitch levels for unaccompanied singing. Tessitura also is a determining factor in solid intonation; a high tessitura is particularly troublesome for most choirs.

Visible Problems of Singers

Directors can eliminate some intonation and/or vocal problems for singers by simply observing them. With volunteer choirs, especially those having many older singers, the conductor needs to be discreet in pointing out these concerns. In most instances, visible and audible problems should be addressed privately with the singer. However, a few minutes spent in a rehearsal doing group activities in an effort to reduce some of these problems can bring about significant change. Conductors should watch for poor posture, a protruding jaw, chin turned up—chin turned down (alto/bass especially), raised or hunched shoulders, singing with a blank expression, a wrinkled forehead, a tongue which rises up in the back of the mouth, bulging neck muscles, a flushed face, music turned to the in wrong place, and the singer not ready on time. Most of these troubles can be corrected easily.

Audible Problems of Singers

The sound of the choir is of primary concern. Congregations may not understand correct musical stylistic interpretations for Renaissance or Baroque for example, but they do have an image of beautiful sounds. Most congregations are less cognizant in matters such as vibrato vs. purity of tone, than in emotional response and clarity of diction. For them, message and sensitivity are at the heart of church music. Yet, for directors, choral sound, must be considered, and can be improved with minimal effort. Barbara Harlow, head editor and publisher of Santa Barbara Music Publishing, tells of her work in a substitute situation for a church choir. She says, "I at last had a chance to change the harsh sound of the sevenfold Amen sung after the prayer which always threatened to jolt me out of the pew! I told the choir that in this instance, purity of tone was everything; after all, the congregation already knew the text. The minister noted the difference to the congregation and said he had been moved!"

Areas often requiring attention are nasality, a sound lacking nasal resonance, hooty sounds, a tight/pinched sounding tone, guttural or strident quality, excessive tremolo and/or wobble, lack of intensity, and fear that normal vibrato is bad.

See Chapter Nine on resources for solutions to these and other vocal problems. Directors with minimal vocal experience will need greater depth of understanding than can be included in this book.

Tips on Choral Tone

For most choral musicians, the sound of the choir is at the heart of their success as conductors. Beauty of sound is an individual matter, and as suggested in the chapter by Howard Swan in *Choral Conducting, A Symposium*, there are, at least, five basic approaches to choral tone/sound/singing. Usually, volunteer choirs establish an unfocused tone, and in many cases, that sound changes from week to week, depending on who is there on any given Sunday. Nevertheless, it is possible to modify a choir's sound through various manipulations. Listed below are suggestions for quick results in developing the choral tone.

a. Start vocalizations from the top down. When the vocal cords are rested after the breath a higher energy results. Lower notes usually need a more relaxed breath so singing them at the end of the phrase/exercise happens naturally. Focus directly on tone by having them sing with eyes closed.

b. Downward "sirens" starting with high pitches are an excellent beginning to any warm-up period. Using an open throat with expanded breath intake will quickly warm the vocal mechanism.

c. Use jaw and mouth relaxation exercises such as making funny faces; this also creates laughter which tends to relax everything. Face loosening exercises also help relieve rehearsal tension.

d. Practice singing a decrescendo on upward scale lines to reinforce understanding that high/loud is not always desired. This will increase breath support habits.

e. Physical exercises involving head/neck movement are useful as warm-ups and as tension relief later in the rehearsal. Posture plays a key role in tone production. Sitting and standing properly is imperative to producing good choral sound.

f. Avoid excessive extended soft singing at the start of any warm-up period. This requires additional energy. After brief soft exercises, quickly move to an activity which establishes a full tone so that singing with proper resonance occurs.

g. Try telling the choir to sing the tone in color. For

example, "this phrase needs to give the music the feeling of shimmering gold" (hot red, warm velvet, etc.). Often this rehearsal vocabulary is more effective with the non-trained singers. Also, singers usually respond to sounds of instruments: basses create the sound of a cello; men try to create the color of a brass choir.

h. SOPRANOS: Over singing is a common problem; strive to have them sing as a section instead of a group of soloists. Special work is needed to help them "lighten" their high notes; singing softer at first helps, but producing a full sound without forcing is an ultimate objective.

i. ALTOS: Church choirs often have an abundance of altos who are older women whose stamina for using their upper range has disappeared. They sometimes feel they are not being heard which leads them to a lazy vocal production. Their mid-range dominates the notes they sing so development of their chest voice is vital to their making a pivotal contribution to the choir's tone color.

j. TENORS: Typically, a shortage of tenors is a church choir predicament. Although the use of alto-tenors is not encouraged, it frequently is an end result. The director should not request altos to sing tenor, but when women want to sing that low, it probably is best to permit them to do that for short periods of time. As with sopranos, tenors should strive to lighten their tone. Using falsetto with a mix of chest voice will help establish a lighter sound that blends.

k. BASSES: They enjoy the low rumbling notes, but need to work on their head voices to reduce the basic thickness of their tone. Basses overly modify their vowels when singing near middle c. Exercises to help

Rehearsals

them learn to sing over (through) their break will give the choir a more even tone color.

Robert Shaw, one of America's most influential choral conductors explained tone to his choir in the following way:

> "One spends the better part of one's vocal education acquiring a 'line,' 'linking the top to the bottom,' 'smoothing out the break'—all of it to acquire a decent, consistent and dependable sound. At the same time, it seems to me that the voices which have the finest techniques also have a wide range of color among their resources. Certainly the chorus is capable of 'bright and dark,' 'reedy and woofy,' 'nasal and throaty.' This is a reasonable request of phrasing. A few minutes of each rehearsal devoted to some phase of their vocal production ultimately will change the choir's sound. A new beauty will emerge; this beauty will be appreciated by the singers and the congregation, and will favorably impact all phases of the worship service."

Twenty Quick Rehearsal Tips

- Train the choir to sing in *commodo* or *recitative* style (freely as in chant).
- Try to hold your hands in a position that forces the singers to look into your eyes.
- When correcting notes, point out wrong **and correct** notes.
- To suggest a difficulty is to create one.
- Avoid over-singing the easy parts and work on difficult passages/problems.
- Minimize singing areas with high or low tessitura to avoid vocal fatigue.
- Elaborate instructions given before starting will invariably be forgotten; when repeating, give them a specific task to focus on, and use "add-on" instructions to increase tasks.

- Always insist that the choir is creating music/art so that nothing is sung as an exercise; even when sight reading, demand musical depth.
- Make your comments dramatic rather than pedantic.
- Avoid vague generalizations and define specific problems (which section was flat or held the note too long).
- Have them sing with their eyes closed so they can listen carefully to the ensemble.
- Try to keep individuals from singing too loud or too soft so that all are equal; this often means having softer voices increase the basic sound.
- Spend time on starting a phrase; exaggerate your conducting, then minimize gestures as you repeat it; eventually eliminate your hands from the process and have them start on a headnod.
- Do not rehearse from beginning to end of a single work; start in different places at each rehearsal.
- Sing without the words, striving to create the same dramatic mood/expression so that the congregation would still understand the intent of the music.
- Have the entire choir conduct short excerpts while they sing; have them also conduct the same material in silence to produce the feeling inside of them.
- Memorize some of the incidental music for the worship services (short amens, introits, etc.) so that they will focus on you and can be ready to sing without using music in places such as prayer responses.
- Correct mistakes as soon as possible to avoid having them become habits.
- Use a baton occasionally if you do not and vice versa.
- Freeze the problem of a difficult passage:
  1. Sing intervals with no rhythm, slowly.
  2. Chant the text in written rhythm OR sing on a neutral syllable.

3. Ask other sections to identify mistakes.
4. When necessary, use light drill on problem for three rapid times in a row to lock in the correction.

Common Rehearsal/Performance Oversights

Directors need to listen and watch for more than the matters of tone, intonation, and musical understanding. The road to the performance is paved with tiny details which many times, are overlooked. The attention to musical/performance details raises the quality of any choir by one level. Correcting the ten faults listed below will produce immediate positive outcomes:

- dropping final consonants
- scooping and slurring notes
- cutting off the ends of phrases or losing intensity at the end of a phrase
- rhythmic instability
- uniform vowel production
- balanced dynamics throughout all sections
- precise attacks of consonants
- watching the director in key places of the music
- holding up the music to facilitate projecting the sound and seeing the director
- taking a breath on the preparatory beat of conductor

Rehearsal Techniques

Throughout this chapter, numerous approaches to improving the sound and performance of choral music have been listed. Most conductors have established their work patterns over a period of years. College conducting classes present useful guidelines for working a composition. Here are a few techniques used by church, community or professional conductors. They are not unusual, but are listed as a reminder to directors; often, we stop using a technique for a long period and it disappears from our library of procedures:

- Chant the text in rhythm focusing on precision.
- Sing a section on a neutral syllable (loo gives most natural beauty) focusing on musical line.
- Freeze a chord to inspect exact intonation of each voice; when needed continue the process for a series of chords, especially those involving half-steps.
- Give the starting cue, then stop conducting and listen, forcing the choir to do all expression and to move rhythmically, in tempo, on their own.
- Have the text read as a dramatic poem without any concern for the music.
- Sing one section at three different tempos and ask the choir which they prefer, and WHY.
- Have the choir sing silently while you conduct and then at various places cue them in/out; this trains their ears to keep track of the sound/line even when they are not singing. This is important for singers; instrumentalists can rest for fifty measures then play their note with little concern for finding the pitch after being out of the texture.
- Have the choir mark suggestions in their score; always have pencils in each folder.
- Have the choir underline important syllables to remind them of a natural stress.
- Make the choir sight read something at every rehearsal.
- Take a few moments to discuss the meaning of the text.

Rehearsal Attitude

The director's attitude toward the rehearsal will spread through the choir and transform them. To be positive, supportive, and energized throughout the rehearsal will instill confidence and bring about irrefutable repair to the music. At times, a smile does more than a statement. Undeniably, people who believe they can do something and have that belief reinforced will be able to do it, if not perfectly, at least better. Attitude is a powerful force in creating a successful choir. Even William James recognized this when he said, "The greatest discovery of my generation is that human beings can alter their lives by altering their attitudes of mind."

CHAPTER 4

> Do not look back in anger, or forward in fear, but rather around in awareness.
>
> James Thurber

REJUVENATION

Webster's *New World Dictionary* definition of rejuvenate is "to make young or youthful again; bring back to youthful strength, appearance." Church music programs constantly need rejuvenation. Rehearsals, activities, types of music, liturgy concerns, and many other features of a successful church music curriculum need constant updating and recharging. The wise director is the one who finds new ways of *doing*.

Motivate the choir members to do their best, to remain active in the choir, and to be a contributor to the overall concerns of the church. This, for many, is more difficult than the day-to-day process of rehearsing/conducting. Balancing the musical needs with the nonmusical needs is a seminal factor in a solid church music program.

Bring new, unusual ideas to the choir and they will revitalize them (and you). Alone, they may seem inconsequential, but woven into the fabric of the total program, they will help form the warp and the welt that makes the design sturdy. Most agree that the more we do, the more we learn. Programs that become too repetitive will stagnate and regress; introducing new events and approaches helps resuscitate forward motion.

"The Dissolving of I" Ceremony

A good choir is one that has a spirit of teamwork. Unlike school choirs, church choirs are comprised of all age groups, backgrounds, and abilities. Molding them into an impermeable, connected collection of singers requires special motivational techniques. One methodology that seems to have an unqualified, persuasive influence is something I use at our first rehearsal of the new season; it is labeled *The Dissolving of I*.

Materials needed are a chalkboard, eight single sheets of typing paper with bold printing to permit people to read them from a distance, and a waste basket. On each of the sheets is printed one of the following words:

INCAPABLE	IRRESPONSIBLE
INSECURE	INSENSITIVE
INCONSIDERATE	IMPASSIVE
IMPOLITE	INDECISIVE

Place the sheets face down on the music stand and begin by offering a few remarks about teamwork. Then start the ceremony by saying,

"This choir is founded on community. We are all in the service of God and the church, and therefore it is important to everyone that we seek to dissolve the feeling of I. So, in this choir no one is to be: INCONSIDERATE."

Crumple the paper with that word and toss it in the wastebasket; then turn and add one mark on the chalkboard.

When each word is spoken and shown, make a few short comments of clarification for each one . Continue the procedure until all items have been eliminated and with that last mark the word WE is completed.

To create a more dramatic effect, place the marks on the blackboard in such a way that the formation of the WE is delayed as long as possible. Marks may evolve as follows:

\, ⊦, \⊦, V⊦, Ʌ⊦, Ʌ Ɛ, WƐ, WE

After completion of this ceremony, have the choir stand, interlock arms, and sing a favorite hymn such as *Lord, I Want to be a Christian* or *When in Our Music God is Glorified*. This could be followed by a prayer and dismissal, so that everyone departs with a strong sense of unity after the first rehearsal. A meaningful block has been laid to the foundation of the choir.

Support Ceremony

This motivational ceremony can be used in many situations, but is particularly forceful just before an important performance. Materials needed are five single sheets of typing paper, scotch tape, and a large pile of thick, hardcover books. Begin with four different colored sheets of paper (typing size). Give one to a singer in each section of the choir (soprano, etc.). Ask them to write the name of their section on the paper. Explain that they can write it large or small, anywhere on the paper, horizontally or vertically. Then, after doing that, they are to return the paper to you.

Take each sheet and roll it tightly into a tube; roll it so that the longest length (11") is achieved, then after making certain it is as tight as possible, secure it by placing a short piece of tape over the edge. Hold up the fifth sheet of paper so that the choir can be reminded about how thin (weak) it is. Then stand the four rolled sheets on end forming four columns in the shape of a book. Carefully place each book on these columns creating one high stack of heavy books supported by the four very thin columns of paper.

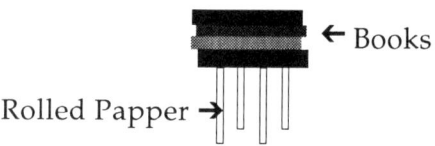

Rolled Papper →   ← Books

Give the analogy of how four sections of singers made of diverse voice colors can work together in support of each other to create a solid foundation in the same way as these thin sheets of paper do when shaped correctly. Creating expressive choral music requires that same kind of support and teamwork. These columns always produce a dramatic example and the picture of those thin papers holding up the books will remain an enduring, vivid image with the choir.

Mini-Advent Concerts

To sing true Christmas music in the worship services during Advent is a liturgical problem. Advent is a different church season; yet in the minds of the congregation, December is thought of as the Christmas season. They, and the choir, want to hear Christmas music during this time of the year. According to the liturgy, Christmastide is that period between Advent and Epiphany. For most churches, this is a time when the choir takes a short vacation after their exhaustive pre-Christmas and Christmas Eve involvement. Thus, they never are permitted to perform much actual Christmas music.

One solution to this plight is to arrange for mini-concerts to be given *prior* to the services during the Advent season. Different choirs (adult, children, handbells) could present brief fifteen-minute concerts as a prelude to Advent services. This gives them an opportunity to perform more of their favorite music without disrupting the formal liturgical requirements of Advent music.

To implement this, the main problem is *training* the congregation to come early and arrive soon enough so that they are not entering during the performance; this is not an easy task, but with yearly reiterations, it does result in a favorable outcome. One of these Sundays could be used as a time for congregational hymn singing of Christmas music; that always seems to have a potent response.

All-Men or All-Women Choir

Changing the sound of the choir occasionally is a simple way of not only bringing variety to the service, but also giving part of the choir a week off. An all-male or all-female ensemble offers a delightful variety to the usual mixed choir heard in churches today. One way of making this particularly significant is to have the men sing on Mother's Day and the women on Father's Day. This gives those being honored an opportunity to sit with their own family for this special commemoration. This is one of those *win-win* situations, as the business world proclaims. Families, the church, and the choir members all receive something from this simple schedule alteration.

Liturgical Drama

Choirs can do more than just sing. Incorporating liturgical drama into the calendar will give it a new burst of energy and perspective. This can take the form of speaking roles, or a combination of speaking and singing used in some form of dramatic cantata setting. The addition of costumes, lighting, and other theatrical elements will make the performance even stronger.

Liturgical drama can be used for those special times such as an evening Maundy Thursday service, or as part of a morning worship service, However, in most churches daylight will eliminate the effective use of lighting, and subsequently cause a loss of dramatic impact.

For Holy Week one possibility is to recreate *The Last Supper* with the men of the choir costumed as Jesus and the twelve disciples. They are introduced individually and come from the back of the sanctuary to take a place at a long table in front; each disciple is described in terms of what is known from Scripture. The women remain in the choir loft and provide the music for that evening. Communion is served to the congregation at the same time as it is taken by the actors. Only the narrator speaks which makes organizing this "scene" very easy. The primary hurdle is the securing of appropriate costumes. In this type of situation, the choir clearly is providing liturgical leadership.

Frozen Tapestry

Another simple, yet practical, type of visual embellishment to services/programs is the frozen tapestry. Here, selected scenes are presented as one-picture postcards. There is no dialogue or movement; the people, in costume and with limited props, are seen in a motionless moment that captures the essence of a larger story. Lighting is needed for blackouts to change the scene. Some common tapestries are the scene at the manger at Christmas, standing at the foot of a cross for Good Friday, or the disciples sitting around a table at *The Last Supper*. This silent, dramatic picture emotionally enhances any anthem sung as background while the congregation views the human illustration.

Caroling

Christmas caroling, once a staple in any choir's activities, almost has become extinct. With new restrictions placed on school choirs regarding the singing of religious music, this ancient tradition now is an unusual community occurrence.

Take your church choir to nursing homes or hospitals, or to visit the elderly during the holidays; this will be an extra special event for them and will provide a personal touch of the season for both singers and listeners. End the evening with a choir social at the church or in someone's home.

Identity

Develop a departmental logo that appears on all music publications. This logo also could be used on choir T shirts/sweatshirts which could be special gifts or for general purchase. Having a "secular" uniform for the group offers many advantages for other kinds of musical performances such as at a church social. Giving the choir a unique identity clearly professes who they are and that they are a team (family).

Summer Music Camp

Most churches hold some type of summer week-long activity for children. This Bible School takes many forms and is particularly appealing to younger ages. Plan a one to five day music camp for choir members and friends of members; children could be taught during the day and older youth/adults at night. The camp would feature interesting group activities such as singing, introductory experience with handbells, and musical games. Start small, perhaps only involving one or two days. Once this event is established it may grow into a week-long annual festivity.

Commission a New Choral Work

Commissioning a new composition is an enterprise that gives any choir a unique, memorable experience. It can have an impact on the entire church. Use a commissioned composition to commemorate occasions such as the dedication of an organ, a sanctuary or a new church, the retirement or installation of a minister, or the celebration of a special time such as the fiftieth anniversary of the church. The church has a long history of supporting the arts. Painting, sculpture, and music have been commissioned/created for centuries. From the Sistine Chapel ceiling and walls to the musical sounds of a new organ, the church has seen the value of including new art as a part of its ceremonial life.

Commissioning a new choral work is a simple process.

The basic steps are:

- establish a fund or donor to pay for the commission;
- identify the composer/musical style which is most appropriate for your church, choir, and occasion;
- contact the composer with an invitation to write for the choir and include a general overview of the type of music you are seeking, the occasion and date for the premier, and a completion date for the composition which will allow the choir adequate time to prepare the new work.

Most composers can be located through their publishers. Contact the publishing company directly and they will either give you a telephone number or address; if, for some reason the composer has invoked total confidentiality, send the letter to the publisher and ask that it be forwarded to the composer. Interested composers will contact the commissioning person/church directly.

Other factors to consider are:

- invite the composer to conduct the premiere, or to attend a rehearsal prior to the first performance to meet the choir and discuss the work (extra fee);
- request a particular text to be set;

- ask that the music have certain features such as a solid organ solo, a brass choir, or an explicit mood such as very festive or quietly introspective.

Be certain that the work will be at the appropriate difficulty level and length for your choir. To commission a work far beyond the performance level of the group places everyone in an awkward situation. Another concern is the way the manuscript is delivered to you for performance. Today, with new technology, most composers use computers for their manuscripts. This facilitates music reading and makes the music much easier to perform. Establish the form of the finished product as part of the commission.

Costs for commissioning a new composition vary according to the reputation of the composer, the length of music requested, and the forces involved in the composition. A work for choir and orchestra requires more time/effort than one for choir and organ, and the same is true for a cantata compared with an anthem. Major composers with significant national and international reputations will expect a high honorarium. All of these implications must be considered when commissioning a composition. As a broad guideline, anthems generally cost from $500-$1500; cantatas and other extended works proportionately move upward from that; again, keep in mind WHO is being commissioned since that is the major factor in the fee expected.

To have a new work created just for your choir/church and to have the privilege of giving its premiere, is an experience that is far too uncommon with church choirs. Certainly, commemorating an occasion with a new anthem and having the direct contact with the composer will be something long remembered by everyone. Finally, when the work is published, the choir's name and dedicatory information will be included at the top of the printed score. This makes their contribution to the church something which reaches beyond the local area, and gives it an enduring quality.

Contemporary Services

In recent years, contemporary services focusing on nontraditional formats, have become very popular, especially with younger people. These services usually use a more *popish* kind music with electronic guitars, synthesizers, and drums. The entire service is loosely structured so that a greater informality is stressed.

Some churches develop this kind of approach to religion to serve a certain subgroup within the church. Although a more secularized music is not encouraged, it is important that the church director be involved to insure quality control. A smaller ensemble can be developed from *within* the choir devoted to such styles as gospel or contemporary Christian. Often this genre of worship can be a help in developing youth choirs; this may be its most value to a music program.

Even if no special service exists, the director may want to develop a youth choir through this avenue of music. They can participate in various church activities and offer another dimension to the total design of the curriculum.

Mardi Gras

The choir, in conjunction with other areas within the church, could host a Mardi Gras festival. Mardi Gras or Shrove Tuesday, is a celebration held on the eve of Ash Wednesday as a last burst of eating and frolicking before entering into Lent, a time of serious contemplation.

These traditional festivals within a church emphasize fun and include such components as jazz music, parades, costume contests, and creole food. They can provide a wonderful midwinter celebration for a church. Since music plays a key role in any New Orleans orientation, unique opportunities are provided for choir members

Providing these kinds of events is prerequisite to success. Cultivate a sense of family within the choir and the church; togetherness or belonging is a cardinal hallmark of recruiting and retaining members.

CHAPTER 5

> To everything there is a season, and a time to every purpose under the heavens.
>
> *Ecclesiastes 3:1*

Repertoire: Part One
THE CHURCH YEAR

The Christian year is divided into six basic time periods of varying length. Within those areas there are numerous specific days associated with the period. In many cases, the exact calendar day changes from year to year. For example, Christmas always remains on December twenty-fifth, but Easter shifts each year because, historically, it is based on the lunar calendar. Early Christians celebrated Easter on the same date as the Jewish Passover. Later, at the Council of Nicaea in 325 A.D., they changed the time of observance to distance themselves from Jewish practices. Ironically Easter derives its name from the pagan Anglo-Saxon goddess Eustre, governess of the vernal equinox.

There is a common plan for the church year which is used by most churches; this schedule is called a lectionary. The Revised Common Lectionary is based on a three-year cycle and provides churches with scriptural passages for Sunday use. Each Sunday has assigned scriptures in the following categories: Act of Praise (Psalms), Old Testament , Epistle, and

Gospel. Churches and ministers follow these readings to various degrees, some very strict and others very lenient.

The broader areas of the Christian year are: Advent, Christmastide, Epiphany, Lent, Easter, and Pentecost/Post-Pentecost (often called Ordinary Time or Kingdomtide). The latter category is the longest with twenty-three to twenty-eight Sundays depending on the cycle. Each period has designated colors to be used by the church on the altar and in other key places. Many choirs use robes that have stoles with these colors giving an even stronger coordination to the seasons (purple-Lent or green-Kingdomtide.)

Each church choir develops a repertoire that usually includes five to ten settings the choir expects to sing *each* year. These favorites may be ancient war-horses such as Handel's *Hallelujah Chorus*. The director is advised to rotate these popular choices into new time-slots such as those during the summer when the choir is not a regular contingency. The nature of the music and its appropriateness to the lectionary determines usability. General guidelines for each season are discussed below, and while most directors understand these seasons, ancillary thoughts are included which may provide new insights into them. Several music publishers such as Augsburg Fortress and Concordia offer church year calendars with recommended text-grouping anthems.

Advent

The Christian Year begins with Advent, a period of four weeks before Christmas. Celebration of this season started in the fourth century in the Gallican region (France and Spain), but not until the sixth century in Rome. The spirit of this season is to develop hope, anticipation and preparation for the arrival of Christ. As with all of the church year, there are specific texts and messages to be conveyed and pondered. Too often, as the month of December unfolds, the texts and music presented by the choir cross over into Christmastide. This, somehow, reduces the magical impact of Christmas Eve and tends to hasten the *"overkill"* most Americans feel during this season.

Advent texts are often highlighted by the *Magnificat*, the song of Mary (see Chapter Seven: Genres). Another common featured text is that of *Gaudete* which is most often used on the third Sunday of Advent. Generally, Advent music focuses on anticipation of the birth of Christ; typical texts and/or melodies include: O Come, Emmanuel; Wake, Awake, for Night is Flying; Now Come the Nations' Savior; and, Lift Up Your Heads, O Ye Gates (also appropriate for Palm Sunday).

Many churches use one Sunday for their annual *cantata*. Instead of singing something for Advent, they usually perform a Christmas cantata. If possible, directors should be attentive to the differences of Advent and Christmastide and use only Advent music *within* the worship service. Emphasis should be kept on the promised coming.

Christmastide

The celebration of the birth of Christ did not begin until about the fourth century; in the early church, faith was grounded in the resurrection. The church's Christmas season is quite short, only twelve days; the ancient song, *The Twelve Days of Christmas (a partridge in a pear tree)* is an acknowledgment of this period. Generally Christmastide begins on Christmas Eve/Day and extends up to January 6, Epiphany. Choir exhaustion is likely by the end of the Christmas Eve services, so, for the following Sundays it is advisable to arrange for soloists/guests to provide the service music. The choir deservedly has earned a rest! Directors have little trouble finding Christmas music. Texts are obvious; carols are popular. One approach to this season is to identify the various parts of the Christmas story such as the birth, the shepherds, or the angels, and to assign one choir to concentrate on music whose text expresses that phase of the story. This is especially helpful for those churches presenting an annual concert of Christmas music. With a narrator reading passages from the Bible prior to each phase of the story, a well-rounded picture of the season can be achieved.

Other suggestions:
- Hold an all-church carol sing.
- Put the choir in the aisles during the singing of carols to give change to the process.
- Dance the carols as originally intended from the medieval times. (see Genre chapter).
- Add new, colorful items to the regular robes.
- Have a singing Christmas tree. (see Rejuvenation chapter)
- Plan the annual seasonal cantata for Epiphany, after Christmas, so that the musical activity does not peak before Christmas, but rather after it when the singers may be less tired.
- Include simple, easy music in the Christmas repertoire; the tendency is to perform challenging music with additional instruments since this season will have the largest congregation and directors want to "show off" the choir.
- Be sure to have at least one "Blizzard anthem" in the church library that could be pressed into service on a snowy or rainy Sunday when few singers are available. (Warm climates need an easy, reliable setting for immediate use, but for a different reason than snow!)

Epiphany

Epiphany is a celebration held on January 6, commemorating the revealing of Jesus as the Christ, particularly in terms of the Magi in Bethlehem; it is sometimes referred to as Twelfth Night. There are several separate associations of Epiphany with the visit of the Kings as the most recognized. Others include Christ's baptism and Jesus' first miracle at Canaan. The manifestation of God in Christ is the oldest feast associated with Epiphany; this dates from about the third century.

Epiphany's last Sunday precedes Ash Wednesday. There is an ancient custom in the Christian church which dictates that since during Lent, *alleluia* is not sung, that there be a *farewell to alleluia* on that final Epiphany Sunday. Churches can commemorate this in many ways; however, Donald Busarow's setting titled *Farewell to Alleluia* (Concordia Publishing, 98-2995) for choir, organ, and oboe, provides a wonderful reminder to everyone. Other ideas are to use *alleluia* in each phase of the service (Introit, Prayer Response, and Benediction) to emphasize its final use.

Lent

Originally, Lent referred to the lengthening of the days in the spring and was derived from the German word *lenz*, but for most people in the Christian world, it is the period of forty days from Ash Wednesday to Easter. Lent observes Jesus' fasting in the wilderness and, usually, is a time of reflection and penitence with the service music following these moods. For some church ensembles, Lent is a troublesome season. Difficult influences include the combination of the sadness of the textual references, the oppressiveness of the weather, and in many areas, the usual exhaustion from the long winter which inevitably reduces choir size.

Lent and Holy Week move through diverse places such as the desert, the city, Golgotha, and finally the tomb. Lent's messages often are less singular. The texts sometimes tend to be more cryptic. For example the Lenten carols, *White Lent* and *Mothering Sunday*, require careful reading to attain understanding. The latter refers to a nineteenth-century custom of having children who had left home, return to visit their mother on the fourth Sunday in Lent; at least one child would take care of the house, allowing the mother to be free to attend church. More common texts, however are concerned with learning the lessons of Christ. Lent is a time of waiting. W.H. Vanstone, in *The Stature of Waiting*, points out that:

> "He went to the Garden of Gethsemane to wait upon the outcome. Waiting can be the most intense and poignant of all human experiences—the experience which, above all others, strips us of our needs, our values, and ourselves."

Waiting demands faith, so Lent provides that period of time for congregational reflection. During this waiting period, our responsibility as church musicians is to help the congregation in their contemplations. Choose music which personalizes the meditations. We know that with Christ's death, resurrection is inevitable; the waiting is ended and hope is answered. Therefore, use music that concerns personal, broader, inward matters to focus on reassurance rather than negative despair. Seek a balance between traditional Biblical messages (the past) and personal needs messages (the present). The congregation probably will not notice your structure, but they may subconsciously feel it.

Passiontide (Holy Week)

The end of Lent is sometimes called Passiontide. This is the most galvanizing single week in the church. Unlike Christmas which is preceded by weeks of consistently joyful anticipation, Holy Week implores a whole panoply of emotions stretching from abject desperation and sorrow, to climatic and overwhelming exultation on Easter morning.

Repertoire: The Church Year

This wide divergence of feeling dictates more than just a casual choice of repertoire. The music must trace the season of penitence through the capture, trial, persecution, crucifixion, and ultimate resurrection, a formidable task. Very focused texts are needed. However, Palm Sunday is also Passion Sunday in the church, and this presents a problem in the twentieth century. Today, the church focuses on that Sunday from the standpoint of the entrance of Christ and the waving of palms (usually by children processing and/or singing in the aisles of the sanctuary—this may be done during a congregational hymn). By doing that as an entrance introit/hymn, time still remains to focus on the other passion areas.

The Passion has a long history which can be traced back at least to the fourth century when parts of it were read or recited in a somewhat dramatic character. In the eighth century, speaking was common, although the words for Christ were sung in plainsong. Later, each of the Gospel stories was assigned to a specific day during Holy Week.

The concept of roles was emerging by the beginning of the thirteenth century when the Passion story was presented by a narrator or evangelist, Christ, and the crowd. Christ was cast as a bass singing in a slow tempo, with the crowd singing in the upper register and faster, and the narrator in a middle range and a generally moderate tempo.

England gave us the earliest known examples of polyphonic PASSIONS which date from about the middle of the fifteenth century. Since then, the story has been set in many forms, such as the dramatic Passion, the motet Passion, the simple homophonic Passion, and, later, the fully developed Passion, which led to the Oratorio Passion. Contemporary composers have been greatly influenced by this story.

Today's churches usually condense the story so that the musical version may last only a short period of time unless a special service is held where extended musical setting is possible. Composers still write extensive settings, but more common are short anthems featuring one special part of the story. Each day has an official passion Gospel, although they are less observed musically than in the past. Assigned texts are:

> Passion Sunday, Matthew
>
> Holy Tuesday, Mark
>
> Holy Wednesday, Luke
>
> Good Friday, John

Passiontide is tragic in character; each incident is teeming with emotion and the wearisome chain of occurrences finally ends on Good Friday.

Holy Week is an exhaustive week for the choir. There may be a special service on Maundy Thursday and/or Good Friday; each reduces preparation time for the glorious Easter music when the church will be filled to capacity. Many churches mark Holy Week with some kind of concert which may present something such as a *Requiem* or *The Seven Last Words of Christ* . Even though a concert is fitting to the mood of the week, prudent planning is required so that all phases of the week will have attention. Time must be saved for rehearsals for the numerous Easter morning services.

Easter

Easter, the capstone of the Christian year is a culmination of everything preceding it; that Sunday morning always demands exciting, festive music, usually with extra instrumentalists included. Directors need to "contract" community players early to insure availability since almost every church will be seeking them.

The Easter season varies in length, but generally lasts about seven weeks. In addition to its opening high point, the other significant Sunday during this period celebrates Ascension. Ascension is a higher priority in the Catholic church. For many Protestant congregations it has become a time of relative unimportance, and when not on a Sunday, is overlooked. This provides a special opportunity for the choir to be leaders by acknowledging this event through music. *God Is Gone Up* is a typical text for this Sunday and there are many settings of it.

One problem is that after Holy Week/Easter, the population of the choir frequently fades. With the warmer weather, the increase in outdoor activities, and the normal spring attitudes, church choirs often suffer depletion. Sensible planning is important. Select music that contributes to the season of Easter without overly taxing the choir.

Pentecost and Post-Pentecost

Pentecost is a significant day in the life of the church year. It occurs fifty days after Good Friday (Pente); in some Anglican churches it is referred to as *Whitsunday* or *Trinity Sunday*, although this is less common in America. Pentecost is the birthday of the church, the time which recalls the descent of the Holy Spirit upon the Apostles; it is marked by the famous chant *Veni Creatus Spiritus* which has been adopted by many Christian churches as the Hymn for Pentecost.

The dramatic character of Pentecost offers opportunity for inventive programming. For example, Richard Felciano's *Pentecost Sunday*, for choir, organ, and electronic tape explores notation and sounds. Symbolically the music accentuates the wind through synthesized utterances on the tape. Even though this kind of avant garde music may not immediately be accepted by singers or congregation, with intelligent preparation, it will be effective. Ask the minister to focus on Pentecost in his sermon prior to the anthem's performance; educating the congregation as to how appropriate this setting is to the true meaning of Pentecost will help them in their perception of the music and the event. Of course there will be those who are disturbed by a radical, dissonant composition, yet, awakening them to the power of Pentecost is part of the true message.

The season of Pentecost continues from that opening Sunday to the day before the First Advent Sunday. Within this season the church experiences World Communion Day, Stewardship Day, Reformation Sunday, All Souls (Saints) Day, and secular observations such as summer vacation, the Fourth of July, the return to school, and Thanksgiving Sunday. Reformation recalls what William Manchester refers to as *The Shattering*, the break from Catholicism and the formation of the Protestant church. All Souls Day is the day to remember those who have died, particularly in the past year. *Secular* observances during this period include Mother's and Father's Days, so there are numerous chances for diverse types of music which may or may not directly connect to the Lectionary.

The last Sunday of the Pentecost season is called Christ the King Sunday. Some churches recognizes this with more emphasis than others. Depending on the normal calendar, this day frequently coincides with Thanksgiving Sunday, reducing its impact on the congregation and the choir.

As mentioned, some church denominations strictly follow the lectionary, others use it as a loose, shadow outline. The denomination and its traditions determines this direction. If the minister's sermons conform to specific lectionary texts, then the music should do the same; if the minister is not guided by the lectionary, then the music director needs information on the sermon topics. Generally,

Repertoire: The Church Year

in those cases where the lectionary is not followed, conspicuous coordination does not happen. The music director must organize the music at least a month in advance; if the minister does not determine the sermon topic (and Scripture) until the week it is given, then proper linkage will not occur. In these instances, following the lectionary is still recommended because other service parts may, indeed, relate to the music. Not following the lectionary loses the symbiosis which makes the service most meaningful.

Coordination between minister and choir director is a portentous phase of a successful worship service. A unified service provides deeper meaning and understanding for the congregation, in the same way a perfectly structured lecture does for an audience. Emphasizing the minister's thoughts with music gives the congregation not only a cognitive awareness, but also an emotional affirmation. John Cage, one of America's most fascinating composers reminds us that,

> "Music is edifying, for from time to time it sets the soul in operation. The soul is the gatherer-together of the disparate elements, and its work fills one with peace and love."

The choice of music for the choir will be a powerful force in helping the weekly service to be a lasting, valuable contribution to the congregation. They will come to know the immediate, daily routines of life, and, at the same time, to understand the cycles of the church and its traditions.

CHAPTER 6

> Music is an experience; experience molds about a third of our total character, judging from psychological studies; therefore, some portion of this proportion of our character traits is the result of the music we hear.
>
> David Tame
> *The Secret Power of Music*

Repertoire: Part Two
VARIETY

At some point, possibly yearly (!), church choir directors will find themselves caught in a maelstrom of controversy about their choices of repertoire. Naturally, we can never please everyone all of the time, but the challenge is to please everyone some of the time. The repertoire balancing act among minister, congregation, choir, and director is one of those thorny problems we all face.

Serious composers write their music to please themselves. Often their style is an enigma to those who hear it. Even among the cultured, an evening of Schöenberg, Ives, or Wuorinen will be a time of little appreciation.

The director's purpose is to enhance the moment of worship, to make it possible for it to be deeper, more meaningful. For many, it may be the only hour of the week when worship takes place. So, if they dislike classical music such as that by Bach or Brahms, we may be negating their moment of worship by performing that style. Yet, if one is to develop an excellent church choir, then the conductor must attract solid musicians with background and training, and usually they are less interested in performing the easy, surface literature often found today in churches.

Furthermore, the minister has a musical agenda which may conflict with congregation and choir. And finally, the director, the one who comes to the worship service as a professional and as an enhancer, brings the strongest background and must follow her/his own conscience of what is right. Church choir directors should develop a working formula for their individual situations. Attach desired percentages to the categories you select. Basic divisions could include the following

- quality historical literature (Bach, Mendelssohn, etc.)
- surface anthems (OK church music with useful message)
- folk, spiritual, music (immediate congregational positive response)
- solid new church anthems
- avant garde literature (music with electronic tape, harsh dissonances, unusual sounds)

Each of these areas has a place in today's churches. Finding a balance is the difficult task. The churches that do only one or two of these divisions throughout the entire year are depriving their congregations of religious and musical perspective. Addressing the needs of everyone, including ourselves as professionals, is vital to attracting new choir members and retaining old ones. Directors should be reminded of the following thoughts:

- Set a goal for the number of new works your choir will learn and perform, and then try to increase it each year.

Repertoire: Variety

- Use canons and the special materials found in the hymnal.
- Develop a swap-list with another church director with indications of those anthems that gave his/her choir and/or congregation a very positive response and those that were perceived as more functional.
- Use hymns as introits and benedictions while establishing a diverse collection of incidental music for the services.
- When repeating an anthem from the previous year (or even sooner), use it as an offertory or in some other way within the service rather than as main selection.
- Sing a simple hymn from the hymnal using a soloist(s) for some of the verses. A structure might be:
  - verse one—full choir in unison
  - verse two—solo with organ accompaniment
  - verse three—soprano section on melody with choir humming individual parts
  - SATB setting of the hymn
- Include a mixture of familiar and unfamiliar texts in your anthems and do the same for musical content so that there is representation of the known and unknown.

Significantly, church directors must consciously design variety into their repertoire choices. Keep an accurate log and plan ahead. If there is a tendency to move toward those works which will be easy to learn, soon the choir will fall into a stale pattern. Both singers and congregations want and need variety in their liturgy; the director is responsible to organize and attain that goal.

Choir directors are urged to devise their own realistic expectations for a complete year and to program toward them. Regrettably, many church directors fail to structure a large, comprehensive program of repertoire. With a working formula such as the one below, choirs are exposed to a wide contrast of musical styles making participation each week more interesting.

Exact numbers will vary according to the involvement of the choir. For example, singing both an anthem and an offertory permits broader coverage of repertoire. As a starting point for a director, consider this nine-month outline:

- Sing thirty-six to forty anthems, with at least ten new to the choir.
- Employ five with brass choir and five with woodwinds.
- Sing at least five anthems unaccompanied.
- Include two Renaissance, five Baroque, two Classical, three Romantic.
- Include the twentieth century: one very modern, five mildly dissonant.
- Have a reasonable balance of fast and slow tempos.
- Sing fifteen which include vocal solos.
- Have twenty-five new items for incidental music.
- Sing at least three in Latin.
- Sing at least one for women only and one for men only.
- Sing at least two extended multi-movement works (Cantata, Requiem, Magnificat).
- Sing at least one involving handbell choir and one involving children's choir.
- Sing at least one antiphonal setting.
- Sing at least one of each of the following styles: gospel, spiritual, folk, and sentimental.
- Include a yearly introduction to one major genre such as Magnificat, Stabat Mater. (See Chapter Seven.)
- Sing several works using congregational singing with the choir.

Repertoire: Variety

Not all church choirs can attain these ambitious aspirations, but without some sort of structured plan, they certainly will not even come close. Setting out broad repertoire goals for the choir will point them in the correct direction. The primary concern is that directors bring to their choirs a variety of styles and genres which will continue to be a stimulation to them, as well as the congregation. If, as suggested earlier, the director believes that part of the choir's mission is to help preserve the traditions of the church, then educating everyone about and through those musical traditions is imperative.

CHAPTER 7

> If I had the power I would insist on all oratorios being sung in costume of the period—with the possible exception in the case of The Creation.
>
> Ernest Newman
> *The New York Post, 1924*

Repertoire: Part Three
GENRES

The third repertoire challenge for directors is to understand and employ basic genres of church music. Generally, most colleges and universities do not have a course of study which thoroughly trains musicians for church choir work. Too often, those who enter the world of church music have only minimal knowledge of the significance of the church year or church music genres. There are dramatic differences in approach and content between school and church music directors! The need for church directors/leaders who are informed is immense.

To preserve church traditions and use of the music that has come down through the centuries, the director must have knowledge of its evolution. The first step is simply to know the musical genres themselves. The church has spawned many of the choral forms sung today. These genres have a long history and have moved away from being functional church music into forms sung as concert music. For example, more masses, such as those by Mozart, Haydn, and Schubert, are heard in the concert hall than as liturgy, at least in America. European churches have continued the Latin mass tradition for worship; on any Sunday morning it is possible to attend a Catholic service and hear this elegant repertoire.

There are many reasons for America's move away from this more sophisticated repertoire. For Catholics, Pope John XXIII's edict (Vatican II) which discouraged Latin singing in favor of hearing texts in the vernacular, has had a profound impact on music used in the church. The relative lack of significant education and development of dedicated church musicians has been another factor in its demise. People often become church music directors with limited knowledge of the associated traditions.

Taste also has a direct, consequential clash with what has unfortunately come be known as *good music.* Our society's education and development of quality in music has shifted downward. Many teachers, schools, and other influences have lost their ability to instill the need for something deeper in musical taste. The number of orchestras and choirs unable to sustain themselves financially because of a lack of audience, is staggering. It is sobering to think about how our technology has provided possibilities for growth and understanding far superior to the past. People wanting to hear music only a century ago had to attend the concert; now they can purchase a recording or see it on television. The same is true for church; television brings it directly into the home and so attending church is not needed. Our technological age of computers and television is rapidly increasing isolationism. Overt involvement is dwindling; this is reshaping society and will have strong bearing on the church.

Populations in churches are feeling the same diminishing future as serious music in concert halls. The first half of the twenty-first century will be a milepost in these areas. More and more, we are becoming removed from others in the work place; computers, for example, have increased breadth of contact, but have reduced direct, face-to-face involvement. Schools and other parts of daily living are experiencing influential changes which collide with the past. There must be an alteration to this course so that good music, serious worship, and other traditional, meaningful parts of our society are retained. We need to remember that liturgy is designed to move the faithful to thought. Church musicians, therefore, should use thoughtful music which lingers in memory.

Positive signs, while more obscured, do exist. For instance, consider the *Chant* album which has enjoyed phenomenal success; this austere music has mesmerized a generation, possibly more than it did centuries ago when it was the "norm." Choral music is one of the purest forms of expression, and in combination with worship it is extremely powerful. Its beauty, such as that of chant, can transcend time and reach a young people who may be culturally lost and isolated from each other. Yet, this music has been described as dull and repetitive by many people; often music appreciation classes rapidly pass through this historical period of chant with the commentary that it all sounds the same so you only need to hear one example of it! If so, then explain the astonishing sales of the recording. Taste? Level of singing? Or, does the intrinsic quality of the music reverberate and touch?

The point is, that if directors know and use quality music, taste can be affected. Without experiencing quality, how can one be expected to desire it? The church and its music can be a harbinger for improvement, and the resurgent popular interest in unison, Latin chant that is about fifteen centuries old reminds all of us of that.

Genres of Church Music

Genres of church music fall into two broad categories: single movement forms and multi movement forms. Church services in the past often lasted far longer than ours do today. Extended music was welcomed by the congregation. For example, in Bach's church, Sunday services could last several hours, so including a twenty-five minute cantata to help interpret the text of the day was an attractive relief from simply hearing the sermon. Today, the music slot has a typical time limit of less than five minutes, so single movement works dominate. Also, the services are quite different in other ways. Active participation of the congregations in Catholic and Protestant churches is now strongly encouraged. And, less formal services are now held. Thus, the need for special kinds of music such as a Gradual, a Passion, or a complete musical Mass has diminished in many denominations.

Single Movement Forms
Anthem

For general use in many American churches, especially Protestant, the anthem is standard repertoire. The term anthem stems from the Greek *antiphona* or *antiphon* (literally counter-sound). Anthems may be traced back to the Middle Ages, which had Anthems of Our Lady; now we refer to those works as *Marian antiphons*. Today, anthems have a much broader classification and texts reflect a diversity of topics.

The first anthems were written by Tallis and Tye in the late sixteenth century. They were, to some extent, a development from the Latin motet (see below). Because of the religious changes in England at that time, it was necessary to have music written to English words from the Scriptures rather than sing the traditional Latin associated with the Catholic Church and Rome. Thomas Cranmer demanded that not only should the music be in English instead of Latin, but it should have a note for every syllable . They also had to adhere to his injunction that they be rhythmically square with shorter phrases and, at first, less sophisticated than their Latin motet counterparts.

Erik Routley, in *Words, Music, and the Church*, suggests that anthems are designed "to comment topically as it were, on the worship, providing a scriptural bridge between the words of the service and common life for people whose common life was entirely ruled by the church seasons." The placement of an anthem in the worship service varies from church to church. By having the anthem early, it can help prepare the congregation for the sermon or aid in setting a more inspirational mood for the entire hour. By having it after the sermon (rare), it can reinforce the message and underscore the main theme.

Anthems have two classifications: verse anthems and full anthems. A verse anthem was one which alternated solo voices with choir. Full anthems were those sung by choir without solos. Both are still an active style in the Anglican church. Today, repeated refrains often are used; these may be sung by the choir or the congregation, adding another dimension to the style.

The number of new anthems published each year is staggering. Generally they are about four minutes duration. There are hymn anthems based on a well-known tune or text; these are quite popular with choirs and congregations. The general anthem may be celebrative or meditative and sometimes evoke both moods. They are available for all seasons of the church year, with a multitude of accompaniments in numerous voice classifications (SATB, two-part).

Motet

The motet has a long history. From about 1220 to 1750 the motet and the mass were the two most important forms of polyphonic music. Throughout the centuries the genre has gone through transformations, so there is no clear definition of a motet. Each period (Medieval, Renaissance, etc.) revamped the motet to its style and need. Usually they were unaccompanied, in Latin, and based on a text other than that found in the Mass, primarily scripture. This set of characteristics is no longer true and today's motets may even be in English making them indistinguishable from the anthem.

Motets were used as special music in pre-Protestant times. They were used as offertories or communion music. Today they are a major art form sung by school/professional choirs wanting to include early music on a concert. They still are used in churches although their Latin text is a barrier for certain denominations. Strangely, today, Latin motets may be sung more frequently in Protestant than in Catholic churches where they originated. Sometimes motets are quite long and are divided into movements with differing tempos and keys. They have received attention from many of the world's greatest composers and regularly are considered among the finest choral music available.

Hymn

Even though inclusion of the term hymn might seem unnecessary, its context is quite varied. Hymns can be traced to pre-Christian times and originally were a tribute to Gods, heroes and other notables. They were intended to be sung. Hymns have become the standard form of music used in most churches and, most often, are associated with congregational singing.

Their fascinating history includes such personages as Luther and Calvin, and they have been adopted by both Protestant and Catholic religions as a main feature of worship. Hymns may be used in a variety of circumstances and directors should develop a more complete involvement of them. For example, expand the congregation's repertoire by selecting a new hymn as *hymn of the month*. Develop a worship service totally devoted to the background and use of different hymns. Include them on church concerts so that the congregation participates and sings during such places as a processional or recessional of the choir. The music director can have a strong influence in the growth of variety and understanding of hymns.

For a scholarly, in-depth explanation of the background and history of the hymn, Erik Routley's *The Music of Christian Hymns* is highly recommended. National organizations are devoted to hymnology, and all directors should delve deeply into this area of church music. People like hymns and have their favorites; build on that to make your music program grow.

Carol

Carols, especially those for Christmas, are among the most popular type of church music. Originally, they were not associated with Christmas or even with a religious experience, but rather were dances connected to particular songs and the winter solstice. (See also Duncan's *The Story of the Carol.*) Medieval carols are the earliest known and may be seen in Vol. IV of *Musica Britannica*. Others may have predated these, but have not been preserved because, at the time, the congregation did not sing in church. They did participate in para-liturgical functions during great festivals outside. These carols were sung then.

The basic structure of Medieval carols followed a pattern of Burden and Stanza. The Burden was sung by everyone, but the Stanza was more narrative in style and sung by a soloist or small group. The outdoor performances usually had a professional dance during the burden. The other common carol form is the ballad, which merely tells a story from beginning to end; the burdens and stanzas were blended into one long idea.

The Puritans practically abolished the carols because they found them less religious due to their diverse associations. Our modern carols and the tradition of singing them at Christmas dates from the nineteenth century. It was not until 1877 that the custom of holding a service of Lessons and Carols originated.

The *Oxford Book of Carols* (Oxford University Press) is a primary source of information and music. These carols can be used as incidental music in different places in the service such as introits or prayer responses. Another idea is to have them danced as originally intended. A new appreciation for carols will be gained if the congregation learns their history. An excellent resource for that is Doug Adams' *Dancing Christmas Carols* (Resource Publications) which includes background and suggestions for implementation and choreography.

Noteworthy is the fact that carols are not only for Christmas. Although these types of carols have suffered from neglect, there are many which exist for other seasons in the church year.

Additional Single-Movement Genres

There are many other types of single-movement choral settings. Basically they are a derivative of those discussed above. A Gradual, for example, had a specific purpose in the

Repertoire: Genres

church but remains as a motet. A Canticle is a comprehensive designation which includes single and multi-movement genres. Canticle types such as *Magnificat, Nunc Dimittis,* and *Benedictus Dominus Deus, Israel* will be discussed as separate genres.

Concertato and antiphonal music sometimes are called genres, but more correctly are identified as styles. Antiphonal music, that which employs echo techniques from instruments or separate choirs, will add interest to any service. The concertato style also features alternation of types of sound and became a common feature during the Baroque Period. Musicologist Denis Arnold in the *New Grove Dictionary of Music and Musicians* says, "the concertato motet was a composition in which the melody was shared between several voices, these voices also being deployed in various groups to give variety of texture. In Germany this method was used in setting chorales."

During the Thirty Years War when men were not available for singing, churches had to find new ways of providing service music. Composers such as Heinrich Schütz contributed to a vast repertoire of music which involved one or two voices, usually with instrumental accompaniment. These compositions will be delightful additions to any choir and can be used in many ways. They use concertato style. There are numerous twentieth-century settings employing this technique; it is particularly popular with Lutheran musicians.

Multi-Movement Forms
Cantata

The cantata continues to be a significant part of church music, although it does not play as consistent a role as it did in the Baroque when it was included in most Lutheran church services. As with other genres, the cantata has changed through the years, but a reasonable definition of one is: a multi-movement work, for chorus, instrumental ensemble, and soloists which has an average length of about twenty-five minutes. The text is either based on the Scripture of the day or on some basic theme/story.

Important Baroque composers who were highly active in this genre were Buxtehude and Bach. Buxtehude's settings tend to be shorter, simpler, and more immediate than those of Bach. Bach's settings, of which more than two hundred have survived, stretch the understanding of textual concerns with symbolism and less obvious explanations of the message. Rhythmic, melodic, and diagrammatic elements were used to convey images of Satan, angels, and other characters or moods. (See Albert Schweitzer's *J.S. Bach*, pp. 74-122 for a detailed explanation.)

Not all cantatas employ choir; many are for soloist alone with accompaniment. Furthermore, there are secular and sacred cantatas. Sacred choir cantatas usually have four to eight movements with at least two for the choir. Chorale cantatas, especially those by Bach, end with a bold, four-part setting of the chorale melody; here the congregation is expected to join the choir for this final movement. An extremely useful tool for church directors is William J. Bullock's *Bach Cantatas Requiring Limited Resources, A Guide to Editions* (University Press of America), which identifies those cantatas that may be of most immediate use to smaller church choirs.

Sacred cantata (and Passion) composition was less frequent after 1750, but has enjoyed a resurgence in this century. Most churches perform a cantata or some similar extended work at least once a year. Because of their length, careful pre-planning is required so that there is enough time, not only to learn it, but also for it to be included in the hour-long worship service. In many instances, single movements can be extracted and reused at different times of the year.

After Bach, the cantata tended to have a meditative theme and be more accessible to listeners. Most were for special occasions rather than for church year significance. Many of today's cantatas are not labeled cantata by the composer; a hybrid form, with or without soloists, has evolved.

Mass

Certainly, one of the great traditions of western civilization has been the formation, development, and continuation of the Catholic liturgy, the Mass. Throughout the past hundreds of years its texts have been the source of inspiration for composers. While styles have changed, the universality of language has remained. Latin dominated for most of this time; only in the last half of this century has the vernacular eclipsed Latin. With that change came others, some of which have been popular, but not necessarily musically successful. Schubert's *Deutsche Messe*, for example, is an easy, pragmatic setting in the vernacular, but is not a work that truly inspires a depth of musical edification.

Masses generally fall into two categories, Missa Brevis (short and/or reduced masses) and Solemn Mass which is more elaborate in length and compositional style, frequently using full movements for just a fragment of the text.

The mass texts have an inner beauty; they stand alone and often are performed in liturgy without being directly connected to each other. Machaut, the great Medieval composer, was the first to link movements musically so that the service had cohesion. Today's composers continue to write complete masses in which the words and music blend into a whole; but, these works rarely are heard in their entirety as part of the service. Composers sometimes only set individual movements of a mass which then, are published separately. Furthermore, sometime only parts of the mass text sometimes are used, fragmenting the mass even more. This is found not only in new music, but many times editors extract a short section of an early work (Renaissance, etc.). This has led to a true confusion especially among young musicians who do not realize that text parts have been omitted.

The mass is not an exclusive product of the Catholic church; other denominations use those texts as part of their liturgy. Bach, for example, made several Lutheran settings of specific movements in Latin; he also composed the great *Mass in B Minor* and created several Missa Brevis settings.

Portions of the mass are classified by their use. There are those for regular use (Ordinary) and those for special days of the church year (Proper); the latter has, in addition to the regular texts, additional words pertaining to the day or occasion. The basic mass movements in the setting of the ordinary are:

Kyrie Eleison (Lord, have mercy)
Gloria in Excelsis (Glory to God in the highest)
Credo (I believe)
Sanctus (Holy, holy, holy)
Benedictus (Blessed is he who comes)
Hosanna (Hosanna)
Agnus Dei (Lamb of God)

Technically, the Sanctus encompasses the Benedictus and Hosanna; when set to music, each is set as a separate movement with its own tempo and key (often subdominant). The Kyrie text is Greek, not Latin. Early masses, were set in unison as chant, as was all church music for nearly one thousand years.

For liturgical use, directors need to be cautious; check the text to be certain it is complete. Throughout history some composers have omitted fragments of the text (especially in the Credo) which makes that mass inappropriate for liturgical celebration.

Magnificat

The Magnificat is the most well-known canticle. It is Mary's song from Luke 1: 46-55, and has come to be associated with the Christmas season, but it is not exclusive of this time of the year. In both the Catholic and Anglican traditions, it is the principal part of the music of Vespers. In the past, especially the last few centuries, the text has received considerable attention from composers, many creating several different settings of the words.

The, Magnificat or Canticle of the Virgin, has ten verses, but is increased to twelve with the addition of the Lesser Doxology. Originally there were eight Gregorian recitation tones upon which it was sung, but the one most common to early polyphonic treatment was *Magnificat Quinti Toni* or in the *lydian* mode. The earliest example of polyphonic settings of the Magnificat come to us from fourteenth-century England. Alternation of verses between plainsong and polyphony was the preferred manner of performance, and usually the first word was treated alone, no matter what set (odd or even-numbered) of verses remained in plainsong; this treatment often involved long melismatic phrases of exultation.

The Magnificat offers churches a wonderful text and assortment of musical styles for use in the Advent season. Choral history may be traced through its development. The Magnificat is shorter than the mass, suitable to Protestant and Catholic traditions, and was adapted to the changing musical styles and tastes with each new generation of composers. Some Renaissance developments included imitative counterpoint (Festa), mathematical games (Gombert), polychoral (Gabrieli), and parody (Lassus). Stylistically, Lassus stands as one of the most prolific Magnificat composers of all time with exactly one hundred settings, although only a few of those are extant. Palestrina produced thirty-five versions and they all remain for us today.

In the Baroque period, the Magnificat continued to flourish, and the addition of orchestral instruments gave it a new character. There have been many recent modern editions of these works. Some of these editions which deserve attention from choirs are those by Leo, Charpentier, Martini, Praetorius, Durante, Galuppi, and an excellent, very useful, and highly recommended setting by Giacomo Perti (ed. Richard Bloesch). Eighteenth and nineteenth-century composers set the text less frequently than those of earlier periods. Haydn has many motets of praise to Mary, such as his *Litanae de B.V.M.* in C, but did not write music for the Magnificat. Some nineteenth century settings, such as those by Schubert, Mendelssohn, and S.S. Wesley exist. The emphasis at that time clearly was moving toward the works by composers writing for the Anglican church such those by Edward Elgar.

British composers continue to dominate the field in this century. Since 1900 there have been over seven hundred published settings of the Magnificat by British composers including such significant writers as Vaughan Williams, Stanford, Howells, Walton, Tippet, Lutyens, and Mathias. For some unknown reason Britten never set the text. Because the majority of these settings are intended for service use, they are most often published with the *Nunc Dimittis*, since those are the prescribed texts for the Evening Service. American composers have set this text with some degree of frequency. A few notable names include Rorem, Pinkham, Berger, Diemer, and Hovhaness.

The Magnificat text appears in the Lectionary cycle. A performance idea is to feature one Magnificat on each of the Advent Sundays, choosing settings from different periods and styles. These repetitions bring home the universality of the story to the congregation and serve as an educational tool for everyone.

Te Deum

Another famous text which has received considerable musical setting is the *Te Deum Laudamus* (We praise Thee, O God), also known as *Hymn of Thanksgiving*. Misattributed to Saint Ambrose, some musicologists have argued persuasively that it may have been adapted by St. Cyprian as early as 272 A.D., although Bishop Nicetas of Remesiana usually is given credit for it in about 400 A.D. Leonard Ellinwood, in *Church Music in History and Practice,* points out that, "The Jewish musicologist, Arthur Friedlander, has identified this melody as being essentially the ancient cantillation of Zechariah XI:10."

This canticle evolved from plainsong into a regular segment of the Anglican Morning Prayer, but it was not until *The Hymnal 1940* that its proper form was finally supplied for universal use. Although the Magnificat perhaps has a greater importance in the Catholic religion, the Te Deum also has maintained a position of significance and use.

Renaissance composers such as Palestrina and Anerio employed the original plainsong melody in their polyphonic settings, but many others later used only the text and have developed free compositions which use orchestra, soloists, and large choruses. Often, this text of thanksgiving has been adopted for settings outside services. These compositions usually are associated with celebrations of great victories or other occasions of gratitude.

Major composers have often set this text for extremely large performance forces. The Berlioz *Te Deum* of 1855, composed for the Paris Exhibition, stands as one of the most exciting; this extended setting far exceeds use in any situation other than as a concert work. Its multiple choirs, multiple brass groups and level of difficulty are an immense challenge. The fine settings by Purcell and Handel are more suitable for church choirs.

Stabat Mater, Ave Verum, Seven Last Words of Christ, and Requiem Mass

The Stabat Mater also has a long and varied history in church music. This story of Mary sorrowfully standing at the foot of the Cross has a text which dates from the fourteenth century. It became a *sequence* with frequent use a century later and has received musical settings by important composers such as Palestrina, Caldara, Bononcini, Mozart (K.33c, lost), Schubert, Dvorak, Liszt, Verdi, Poulenc, and Penderecki.

Less common as formalized liturgical music, the Stabat Mater is most often seen as concert music, particularly because settings tend to be long and involved. Schubert's two settings are shorter and more suitable for church choirs; although they do require instrumental accompaniment, they could be played on organ alone. The numerous musical treatments of Stabat Mater, Ave Verum Corpus, and The Seven Last Words of Christ have become standard repertoire for Good Friday concerts and services. The Ave Verum Corpus is a single-movement motet and Mozart's version is among the most popular church music repertoire used today. Another multi-movement form which is appropriate for this season is the Requiem Mass which includes the sequence

Dies Irae (Day of Judgement). Prior to the sixteenth-century Council of Trent, the liturgical celebration of the Requiem Mass differed from region to region; the Dies Irae did not become a standard addition to the Requiem celebration until the mid-sixteenth century, and then in France. As with the Stabat Mater, by the nineteenth century, the Requiem had become more common to the concert hall. It, too, has hundreds of settings with those by Faure and Verdi receiving the most frequent performances. Verdi's *Requiem* is long, difficult, and generally beyond church use; however, the Faure setting is a common multi-movement work performed by church choirs. John Rutter's recent *Requiem* has received considerable attention from church choirs and is performed frequently.

Passion

The Passion is an important genre that has remained a vital part of worship services. One Sunday a year is determined as Passion Sunday when the story is to be told in some way during the service. Because Passion Sunday is also Palm Sunday, its emphasis has been truncated in many churches.

Traceable, at least back to the fourth century, the Passion is a musical setting of the galvanizing events of Holy Week. Each of the Gospel stories eventually was assigned to a specific day during Holy Week. Unlike Christmas, which is a continual scenario of joyful events, Passion Week is tragic in character, and the story is condensed into seven days instead of several weeks.

Most Passion settings such as those by Schütz, Bach, and Handel, are too long for worship services. To be included, judicious cuts must be made for today's service length. As with other genres, the Passion is most often found as a concert composition. There are many modern, brief Passions such as those by Richard Hillert and John Carter which are quite suitable for service use. Elements of the Passion story also are found in isolated "anthem" settings and in cantatas, which provide shorter compositions that adapt easily into any worship service. These may or may not use soloists to perform the various roles of Peter and Jesus, as was originally intended.

Oratorio

The oratorio is similar to a cantata, except that it is far longer. Both eliminate costumes, sets, and action, and both tend to feature the chorus, while still having solos throughout. Although there are antecedents before the seventeenth century which gave rise to *dramatic* story telling (Medieval Mystery Plays and narrative madrigals), the development of the oratorio is most associated with the seventeenth and eighteenth centuries. Growing from early settings called *Oratorio Latino* by Carissimi and his contemporaries, the oratorio was primarily an Italian genre. Later, through such means as the Lutheran *Historia*, a scriptural story intended for church use, the oratorio spread throughout Germany and incorporated new techniques of style. Because the Passion story was frequently used, a hybrid form, the Oratorio-Passion, evolved.

Musical centers such as Hamburg and Luebeck are credited with cultivation of the German oratorios, but it was in mid-eighteenth century England, with Handel, that the oratorio achieved supreme success. His oratorios, generally in three "acts" as he preferred calling them, solidified the form into the shape most often associated with the genre. Handel's *Messiah* has become the standard work in this genre, and its popularity results in hundreds of performances each year with church, community, and school choirs.

Repertoire: Genres

Oratorio composition continued with excellent settings by Haydn in the Classical Period and in monumental nineteenth-century works such as those by Mendelssohn, Franck, Saint-Saens, Gounod, and Spohr. In the twentieth century, significant oratorios have been composed by Elgar, Walton, Tippett, Vaughan Williams, Hindemith, Debussy, Stravinsky, Messiaen, and Penderecki.

Oratorios may be secular or sacred and are not used as church music in a liturgical sense, but rather they are performed as concert music. Their extended length of over two hours prohibits complete use in a worship service. Furthermore, they require accomplished singers as soloists and in the choir. The difficulty level of most oratorios, particularly those by modern composers, will be beyond many church choirs; however, joint productions by church choirs are common and are recommended for both musical growth and as fund raisers. They give strong visibility to the chorus, have a story which creates audience interest, create opportunities for local or professional soloists, and provide an extension to the normal anthem-length music usually performed by most church choirs.

Benedictus Domine Deus Israel

The Benedictus Domine Deus Israel is another canticle of the Morning Service (Te Deum is the other one). In the Anglican Church this plays a more important role. For a comparison of the Anglican and Roman Catholic service counterparts, see Wiendandt, *Choral Music of the Church*, page 174.

Other Genres

There are many other types of multi-movement works which may be seen as subgroups to those listed above. For example, in this century, the definition of a cantata has become controversial, because composers have expanded its original form. Structures such as sets of music, those having many movements for choir, have become popular. Here, the music is built around a central topic/theme such as winter or around poetry by a single author. Soloists are used as part of a choral movement rather than in extended, solo movements as in cantata and oratorio.

Another type of form used in churches is the concertato which is longer than a single anthem, yet shorter than a cantata. These settings may be based on a single chorale or hymn. They will have divisions within them which function as movements (i.e., changing tempos, performers, instrumentations) each separated by short pauses. Each division is a setting of a different verse of text; many have a *ritornello* (refrain) which recurs throughout.

Musical Groupings beyond Genres

The musical structures already described serve as the basis for most church musicians. The mass, anthem, and cantata are the genres which dominate Protestant and Catholic American churches. However, some less formalized types of groupings also are found in today's churches.

Imaginative music directors look for innovative ways of preserving traditions, stimulating interest, and developing growth in their programs. To simply come together once a week and learn an anthem, which is then sung on Sunday, is no longer acceptable as a productive church music environment. Technology offers a myriad of interesting and challenging activities in schools and home, and has given musicians new impetus to develop their local programs. Boring repetitive rehearsals, music that does not stimulate the mind and heart, and lack of attention to interpersonal relationships will sound a death knell to church choirs. Many of the suggestions given here have been aimed at creating provocative approaches for the choir. Variety in doing is the key element that attracts and retains members. Some programming ideas for consideration follow.

Church Music Survey

Develop a concert that traces the evolution of church music so that both singers and congregation can develop an understanding of the past. Ministers/priests give weekly sermons on ancient Biblical texts and try to translate and relate them to today's society. Only a few in the congregation will have any knowledge about the traditions of church music. This method will provide training through entertainment.

Begin the concert with a *plainsong* and move through different styles associated with each general period such as the Renaissance and Baroque. Use someone from the choir as a narrator; prior to the performance of each selection or style give a brief explanation of the music and its context in the church. The more the congregation knows about church music, the better it is for the weekly services, the choir, and them. Understanding the universality of texts, languages, and styles of music encourages acceptance of diversity within the liturgy.

As a choir director, become a teacher for the congregation. Offer talks to the various Sunday School classes, youth and adult. Give brief, informal presentations to them during their weekly meeting to encourage more interest in the choir's activities. In some denominations the music director can teach a church music history class as part of the confirmation process.

Concert/Service Themes

Concerts (and services) which focus on a single theme move them from mere entertainments to something more substantial. Most churches will have some type of musical event for Christmas or Easter. People come knowing what to expect in terms of the messages.

Plan concerts which celebrate anniversaries of composers. 1997, for example, is the year of the following: Schubert, 200th birthday; Mendelssohn, 150th anniversary of death; Brahms, 100th anniversary of death. Musical commemorations for giants such as these composers will merge those two motivating ingredients of entertaining and education.

In addition to typical seasonal celebrations in the church, organize musical performances around specific types of music or text. To focus on a single element is to illuminate it. For example, singing diverse settings of Psalm 23 throughout the many Sundays in Lent strengthens cohesion within the services. Texts which may not be scriptural, such as those by the wonderful twentieth-century writer, Fred Pratt Green may serve as a catalyst for organized performances in services or concerts. Different arrangements of the same hymn tune or well-known melody will help develop cognitive awareness of its strength or universality.

Find ways of letting repertoire do more than merely be an adjunct to worship; make it a conduit for deeper penetration of conscious awareness. A comprehensive breadth of literature use will strengthen any choir and any church.

Keep track of what music is performed each year to be certain that the choir is reaching out into new styles and composers. Introduce them to the extraordinary as well as the popular repertoire, and their musical and religious experience will be more meaningful. Then, perhaps, Handel's comment to Lord Kinnoull after the first London performance of the *Messiah*, will be applicable to your local church. He said, "I should be sorry, my Lord, if I have only succeeded in entertaining them; I wished to make them better."

CHAPTER 8

> O money, money, money, I'm not necessarily one of those who think thee holy,
>
> But I often stop to wonder how thou canst go out so fast when thou comest in so slowly.
>
> Ogden Nash
Hymn to the Thing
that Makes the Wolf Go

Resources: Part One
FUNDING

As in any arts oriented organization, finding ways to increase basic funding is something that concerns directors. Churches have budgets primarily based on income from the congregation. The size of the church membership determines availability of money, and personal interests within the church provide direction and priority for expenditure.

Most churches feel that music is an important part of their experience, however the *function* of repertoire is often more of a concern than the *quality* of the repertoire. Not every church will have competent musicians willing to give freely of their time on a continual basis as leaders or even participants. Trained professionals, who know the repertoire and have good musical backgrounds to improve vocal and instrumental performance, will be needed to build competent church music programs. Too often, churches feel that they can "get by" with volunteers who have limited experience, so the music area generally continues on the same track of mediocrity. Doing everything as it has been done in the past does not attract new members to the choir or the church unless the quality level that had been established is quite high.

Cheaper is not better in the total perspective of a church music program. Spending money for attractive robes is better than having the choirs sing in their regular clothes. Allocating money for an excellent organist is better than taking a chance that a good one will donate her or his services; competent solo and accompanying organists are rare and they expect to be paid well for their talent and background.

The same is true for adult and children's choir directors; if they are qualified, they expect to be paid. So, at the foundation of the problem is that, in America, the church has not been attracting large numbers of people into this arena as a vocation because full-time employment is limited and part-time involvement has a minimal salary or none at all. Regrettably, the future does not look better. In each community there are a few churches with wonderful music programs. In these instances churches have gone beyond their local constituencies and have hired excellent musicians to guide and participate in their programs. Churches have supported the musicians' suggestions, both musically and financially, and as a result, have continued to grow and prosper in terms of membership. Undeniably, people seeking a new church will make their choices based on the minister and his style of preaching, the children's and/or adult programs within the church, and the music area, which directly connects to both of the other two. Therefore, investing in an excellent music program is, indeed, a wise decision that will continue to reap benefits for everyone.

Resources: Funding

Salaries for the Music Director and Organist

The salaries paid for church musicians have a wider range than those found in other fields such as education. Starting salaries for entry-level teachers in public schools generally range from twenty to twenty-five thousand dollars, depending on the area of the country. There are lower teaching salaries in some areas ,but these figures are typical. Substitute teachers, those used on a onetime, daily basis, earn about fifty to one hundred dollars a day.

Part-time church positions often have a three to eight thousand dollar range for a director or organist for an entire year. Yet, the director/organist for the church will have earned college degrees just as the school choral director. To compound the inequity, in most cases churches require regular evening and weekend responsibilities. For part-time church musicians holding another full-time position, that eliminates time off for a weekend escape; this is a serious detriment to choosing this supplemental career.

Other Salaries

The plight of those directing handbell or children's choirs is even worse. Those directors often earn as little as one-hundred dollars a month since they are not expected to perform each week. They do, however, have rehearsals throughout the month, perform on special occasions as well as during services, and usually spend a considerable amount of time contacting performers with reminders about rehearsals/performances.

Private music teachers charge about twenty to thirty dollars an hour with fees related to the level of the student; lessons are given in the home of the teacher who enjoys tax benefits for the studio and saves time by not having to travel. Many churches base their salaries on a comparison with private teachers and arrive at a dollar amount by a modified-hourly time frame. This does not treat the musician in a fair way because of the considerable additional time that is overlooked in the process. Score study, music searches, and practice time are among the many kinds of necessary preparation for the job that are hidden and not considered. A yearly salary that avoids counting "hours" is a better, more professional approach for everyone. Very good people should be expected to do more and, consequentially, be paid more.

Salary Recommendations

Minimum salaries for the part-time music director and organist should start at one thousand dollars a month each. Yearly increases to at least cover inflation should be a natural part of the contract. Furthermore, merit increases for excellent work also should be apart of any salary package. Part-time positions do not include benefits packages for health and retirement; this also adds to their dilemma. A substantial base salary is required to bring more fine musicians into part-time church work.

Those hired as full-time musicians for the church should expect a minimum entry-level salary of, at least, twenty-five thousand dollars. Again, location in the country will have an influence on the exact figure, but certainly, most churches are not paying their professional people enough. Here, health and benefit packages must be included. The number of organ students in American colleges and universities continues to dwindle. One difficult problem already quite serious is to find and retain good organists for churches. The opportunity to make a good living at this profession is key to this problem.

Paid Section Leaders

Churches often hire singers to serve as section leaders. Having a wonderful, trained voice in each section of the choir greatly improves its tone and sight-reading ability. These people provide musical leadership and reduce the rehearsal time. They also are available for solos within the choir and to help with other needs such as music for weddings and funerals. Music directors who are excellent singers often reserve these additional financial opportunities for themselves; however, in large churches it is rarely impossible for them to have time to do this.

In those places where colleges with music programs exist, set up a scholarship program for music students. Work directly with the college to identify quality students who can be hired as section leaders. This will benefit the college and the church. (The scholarships can help attract good students to the school.) The church, in turn, will be doing something to develop interest in young professional musicians; it is hoped that a large percentage of them eventually will become church music directors. In many instances, students who sing in a church where music is of a high quality and priority may seek directorships in other churches before graduation. Experiencing good music programs is a special training for them; it may be quite different from what they had in their local hometown church.

The Purchase of Memorial Anthems

An easy method of increasing the choir library is to offer opportunities for congregation members to purchase a memorial anthem. The director chooses the music, and when the anthem is first performed at a service, there is a dedication placed in the bulletin below the anthem entry. For example:

> *This anthem was purchased for the choir by Mary Ann Smith in beloved memory of her husband, John, who passed away three years ago this week.*

People also like to purchase anthems for special occasions such as Christmas and Easter. They may be a memorial for a loved one or simply a method of showing support for the minister or the choir; the dedication entry is different, but the result is the same.

This fund raiser requires little effort and can be an effective and valuable method for increasing the number of new works purchased each year. Anthems typically cost about $1.20–$1.35 each (sixty to eighty dollars total depending on the size of the choir). Directors should buy a few extra copies at the time of the purchase to account for growth in the choir and/or loss of music over time. This is a small investment from a congregation member, yet has a lasting value. Each time the anthem is used by the choir, the memorial dedication could be repeated, however, this may eventually becomes cumbersome.

Orchestra Purchase

The use of additional instruments with the choir is highly recommended. Within the church there may be many adult or youth members with competent musical background who are interested in occasionally playing with the choir. Augmenting the accompaniment with solo instruments gives the choir a new sound and usually raises the performance to a new level.

Church budgets generally do not include enough money for orchestra use in worship services. Concerts with tickets may raise enough money to pay for an orchestra on its program. Yet, singing with an orchestra within the service a few times a year places the emphasis of the music program in the proper place. Using a chamber orchestra for worship services clearly underscores the fact that the music program primarily is for liturgy.

In most situations having one string player on a part will adequately balance the choir. Hiring community musicians is costly, but worth the money and time. With proper presentation, it is possible to identify congregation members who are willing to pay for the orchestra in the same way as for the purchase of memorial anthems. A special announcement can be placed in the bulletin indicating this dedication. By choosing works which use limited string parts (Baroque and Classical), cost can be kept to a minimum.

Singers greatly enjoy singing with instruments, especially strings. Their vocal sound is immediately improved, and there is a sense of elegance that surrounds orchestral use in church. Cantatas and Missa Brevis settings/movements, are perfect for adding a small chamber orchestra to the choir. On those Sundays, use the orchestra in other places in the service to capitalize on their being there (playing the hymns and incidental service music, for example).

Some churches have a church orchestra formed from its own members. These instances are less common but are encouraged. Large, musically active churches, have regular instrumental rehearsals and include the orchestra in the worship services. Sometimes these groups are used as a separate church ensemble and not just for accompanying the choir.

Benefit Concerts

Earlier, it was suggested that a MUSIC OF THE CHURCH series be established. These types of concerts which feature musicians from the local church, provide an excellent method for raising funds. When planning fund raising concerts, remember that children generate audiences. Be certain to include the children's choirs as a part of the concert because the audience size will increase proportionately when they are there.

To avoid having the audience shrink during the concert, place the older children's choirs in the sanctuary and have them remain there throughout the concert. Put the youngest children's group near the end of the concert. Have their director hold a rehearsal for them during the concert so that parents must bring the children prior to the start of the concert and then stay until its end. If possible, use everyone for a final, festive composition.

Selling tickets will always generate more revenue than merely passing a collection plate. To assure attendance have the performers sell tickets in advance. This requires more work, but if the main purpose for concert is to raise funds, then it should be done.

Benefit concerts which involve performances by recognized performers are possible. For best results, have the performer's fee underwritten by some person or organization; an agreement could be made to pay back all or part of the sponsor's money from the proceeds. Even with large churches with space for huge audiences, there may not be enough money made to cover all of the expenses, especially if the performer's fee is considerable. An underwriter guarantees that there will be no loss to the church.

Season ticket sales for the series will increase if one or two concerts of a church series feature special guests . Purchase of a season ticket guarantees that people will be able to attend those special concerts. Management of a series always has a balance between those expensive concerts which are sure to be of great appeal, and other concerts that have a less broader appeal, but which do not require as much money to produce.

The annual church musical is an activity that has particular appeal for children's or youth groups. Audiences

Resources: Funding

enjoy the less formal music associated with the musical; it may or may not be based on a religious theme. Raising money is only one goal of this event; attracting and keeping students in the group often is a more important goal. These "shows" are a popular recruiting tool.

Active Budget Appeal

Directors need to take active, highly visible roles in the budget process for the church. Unquestionable documentation should be presented each year which reveals evidence of responsible use of funds coupled with need for an increased budget owing to growth. Often increased cost factors, such as those for new music, are overlooked. As the choir grows, the number of copies of music needed for purchase expands. Without a separate budget line strictly for replacing lost music and/or buying additional copies for new people, much of the church music library can not be used with the larger choir. Preserving and increasing the yearly budget for a church music program will be a struggle. Without mindful attention to this part of the director's role, programs moving forward can be stifled. Success demands more money, energy, and vigilance. Growing programs need increased funding just to stay even, and directors must be persuasive in presenting their budget needs.

Additional Resources

Of course, there are many other ways to raise funds. The sale of candy or fruit, a car wash or a spaghetti dinner, are some typical ideas to produce income. Proceeds are determined by the effectiveness of sales—frequently unsold items reduce the profit margin. These kinds of fund raisers require considerable planning and work, and are recommended only to the most hearty and committed groups. Selling can be very successful or extremely disastrous and should be approached cautiously.

The church, as with almost all institutions in our time, is concerned with raising money to support itself. Raising money through musical means (i.e., concerts, memorial anthems) is recommended over nonmusical projects such as selling candy. Other groups within the church will appreciate it if the music program raises its funds through their talent, because that permits other groups more flexibility in nonmusical fund raising. Budgets will not be sufficient to sustain everything needing support so all church agencies, including music, will have to find ways of securing external funds. This malady is not something peculiar to our century, but has always been around the church. Pope Leo XIII reminded everyone that,

"It is one thing to have a right to the possession of money, and another to have a right to use money as one pleases.""

CHAPTER 9

> Music and religion are as intimately related as poetry and love; the deepest emotions require for their civilized expression the most emotional of the arts.
>
> Will Durant
> *The Age of Faith*

Resources: Part Two
MATERIALS

Today, everyone is inundated with catalogs, brochures, and announcements of materials. Just as telemarketing has driven many to secure unlisted telephone numbers, the overabundance of mailings has caused many to simply throw them away without review. The resource list included in this chapter is not intended to be exhaustive, but rather highlights recommended materials. Directors may start with this very selective list and then pursue additional resources on their own. The list will satisfy those wanting a quick, short reference of useful materials.

ORGANIZATIONS

American Choral Directors Association (ACDA)
502 SW Thirty-eighth Street, Lawton, OK 73505

(most professional organization for all types of conductors: church, school and professional)

American Guild of English Handbell Ringers
601 West Rivermore Ave, Dayton, OH 02215-1401
(useful for handbell choir directors)

American Guild of Organists (AGO)
475 Riverside Drive, Suite 1260, New York, NY 10115
(most professional organization for organists)

American Orff-Schulwerk Association
P.O. Box 391089, Cleveland, OH 44139-8080
(useful for children's choirs)

Association of Anglican Musicians
P.O. Box 37, Pacific Palisades, CA 90272
(primarily Anglican, Church of England organization)

Association of Lutheran Church Musicians
P.O. Box 16575, Worcester, MA 01601
(primarily Lutheran organization)

Christian Copyright Licensing, Inc. (CCLI)
6130 NE 78th Ct. Suite C-11, Portland, OR 97218
(information on copyright use in churches)

Choristers Guild
2834 W. Kingsley Rd, Garland, TX 75401
(useful for children's choirs)

Chorus America
1811 Chestnut St., Suite 401, Philadelphia, PA 19103
(serves all types of volunteer choirs)

Church Musicians National Referral Service
Department 60, Box 36, Huntington, WV 25706-0036
(helpful for church job searches)

National Association of Pastoral Musicians (NAPM)
225 Sheridan Street N.W., Washington, D.C., 20011-1492
(primarily Catholic organization)
National Drama Service
127 9th Ave N. Nashville, TN 37234
(publisher of scripts, books, hints for drama ministries)

PERIODICALS

Creator
P.O. Box 64775, Tucson, AZ 85728
(bi-monthly magazine of balanced church ministries)

The Diapason
380 Northwest Highway, Des Plaines, IL 60016
(international journal for organ, harpsichord, and church music)

Handbells
Music Dept. of Sunday School Board,
MSN 114, 127 Ninth Ave. North, Nashville, TN 37234
(includes articles about and music for handbells)

The Hymn (Hymn Society of America)
Boston University School of Theology
745 Commonwealth Ave., Boston, MA 02215-1401
(history and uses of hymns)

Sing!
P.O. Box 5191, Belmont, CA 94002
(an international newsletter for church choir singers)

Sing! Jr.
P.O. Box 5191, Belmont, CA 94002
(an international newsletter for children's choirs)

Ring
P.O. Box 5191, Belmont, CA 94002
(an international newsletter for church handbell ringers)

BOOKS

A Handbook of Church Music
Carl Halter & Carl Schalk.
Concordia Publishing House. ISBN 0-570-01317-8

Brass Instruments in Church Services
James Ode.
Augsburg Publishing House. ISBN 73-105669

Building the Youth Choir
John Yarrington.
Augsburg Fortress, Paperback, #11-5215

Choir Rehearsal Prayers
Quentin Faulkner.
Morningstar Music Publishers, MSM 90-2

Choral Conducting, A Symposium
Harold Decker & Julius Herford.
Appleton-Century-Crofts. ISBN 72-94347

Choral Music in the Church
Elwyn Wiendandt.
Free Press of Macmillan Co, 65-10187

Hymns and Their Users
James R. Sydnor.
Agape of Hope Publications. ISBN 0-916642-18-6

Resources: Materials

Jubilate!
Church Music in the Evangelical Tradition
Donald P. Hustad.
Hope Publishing Co. ISBN 0-916642-17-8

Jubilate II
Church Music in Worship and Renewal
Donald P. Hustad.
Hope Publishing CO., #1631

The Choral Experience.
Ray Robinson & Allen Winold.
Waveland Press, Inc., 0-88133-650-5

Church Music in History & Practice
Winfred Douglas & Leonard Ellinwood.
Charles Scribner's Sons, CCC 61-13604

Key Words in Church Music
ed. Carl Schalk.
Concordia Publishing House, ISBN 0-570-01317-8

Sacred Music USA - A National Directory & Resource Guide to the Sacred Performing Arts
Sacred Music Publishers 21346 St. Andrews Blvd. Suite 207, Boca Raton, FL 33433
(a comprehensive resource for church music directors)

The Lutheran Chorale
Johannes Riedel.
Augsburg Fortress, CCC 66-26802

The Music of Christian Hymns
Erik Routley.
G.I.A. Publications. ISBN 0-941050-00-9

The Psalter: Psalms and Canticles for Singing
Westminster/John Knox Press

The Second Voice
Devotions for Church Musicians
Morningstar Music Publishers, MSM 90-7(italic

Today's Church Orchestra
George M. Frink.
Carol Press of Hope Music, CB 9003

Twentieth Century Church Music
Erik Routley. - AGAPE, Hope Publishing Co

Words, Music, and the Church
Erik Routley.
Abingdon Press, CCC 68-11479

VIDEOS

The Reason Why We Sing (#631)
Hymn Society Book Service, Boston Univ. School of Theology,
745 Commonwealth Ave., Boston, MA 02215
(Alice Parker demonstrates working with a congregation to improve congregational song)

Yes! We'll Gather (#613)
Hymn Society Book Service, Boston Univ. School of Theology,
745 Commonwealth Ave., Boston, MA 02215
(Alice Parker works with a church exploring old and new hymns and their use)

Daily Workout for a Beautiful Voice
Santa Barbara Music Publishing,
PO Box 41003, Santa Barbara, CA, 93140
(Charlotte Adams' techniques for vocal development)

Resources: Materials

When We Sing (#630)
Hymn Society Book Service, Boston Univ. School of Theology,
745 Commonwealth Ave., Boston, MA 02215
(Alice Parker with composers, poets, and church musicians in discussions of music and faith)

Sing and Rejoice (#618)
Hymn Society Book Service, Boston Univ. School of Theology,
745 Commonwealth Ave., Boston, MA 02215
(Alice Parker demonstrates how to improve congregational singing)

Positive Motivation for the Choral Rehearsal
The Music Mart,
3301 Carlisle Blvd NE, Albuquerque, NM 87110
(Eph Ehly demonstrates motivational techniques)

Evening with Craig Courtney
The Music Mart,
3301 Carlisle Blvd NE, Albuquerque, NM 87110
(Courtney is composer/arranger of church music, and head editor for Beckenhorst Press)

Fine-Tune Your Conducting Skills
Santa Barbara Music Publishing,
PO Box 41003, Santa Barbara, CA 93140
(Timothy Mount's 75 valuable minutes of instruction to improve conducting technique)

What You See Is What You Get, Rodney Eichenberger
Hinshaw Music Inc.,
P.O. Box 470, Chapel Hill, NC. 27514-0470
(Eichenberger demonstrates non-verbal vocabulary and techniques to improve rehearsal efficiency)

POST CARDS

Choir Post Cards (Reminders, missed choir, etc.)
Art Masters Studios Inc.,
2710 Nicollet Ave. South, Minneapolis, MN 55408-1630
(12 different post card choices with cute messages)

COLLECTIONS OF MUSIC

The New Church Anthem Book
ed. Lionel Dakers.
Oxford U. Press, ISBN-0-19-353109-7

The Shorter New Oxford Book of Carols
ed. Hugh Keyte and Andrew Parrott.
Oxford U. Press. ISBN 0-19-353324-3

The Novello Book of Carols
ed. William Llewellyn,
Novello, ISBN 0-853680-127-5

HANDBELLS

Jeffers Handbell Supply Inc.
Carillon Park, Irmo, SC 29063-1728
(comprehensive supply outlet for handbell equipment, music, and gifts)

Malmark Bellcraftmen
Bell Crest Park, Box 1200, Plumsteadville, PA 18949
(quality handbells and choirchimes for children's groups

Schumerich, Carillions, Inc.
Carillon Hill, P.O. Box 903, Dept. CR, Sellersville, PA 18960
(quality handbells and carillons)

Resources: Materials

INTERNET AND COMPUTER

The internet is a rapidly changing resource. It is evolving with numerous daily changes and while we cannot promise that these resources are available, the internet will continue to be a valuable tool for all church musicians, and should be reviewed frequently.

Choral View (on computer disk)
Call 1-800-736-0595
(all choral reviews written by ACDA, AGO, Choristers Guild, The Diapason, AGEHR, and Creator Magazine)

Choralnet
http://www.sdsmt.edu/choralnet
(website for e mail lists divided into Choralist, Choraltalk, and Choral Academe; links to numerous resources for the choral director)

Creator Clip-Art Book, Vol. III
920 S. Roundtail Place, Tucson, AZ 85748
(electronic click art for Apple or MS-DOS)

Ed Wilmington's General Church Music Information
www.getnet.com/-musicmin
(a personal website useful for general information)

Goshennet
http://www.goshen.net
(an internet directory of Christian Resources)

Tempo Music
http://www.gnms.com/tempo
(includes The Worship Network, The Church Musician software, Hymn Search for Windows and other tools)

The Church Music Report
http://www.goshen.net/tcmr
(home for CMReport and other music resources)

Worship and Music Ministry Resouece Center
http://www.getnet.com/-musicmin/
(creative ideas for worship planning primarily in blended and contemporary style)

MISCELLANEOUS

Creator Clip-Art Book, Vol. I,II. & III
920 S. Roundtail Place, Tucson, AZ 85748
(books of clip-art for newsletters, memos, etc.)

CHAPTER 10

> "How many of you know what's important?" Up went all the hands. "Very good," said Stuart, cocking one leg across the other and shoving his hands in the pockets of his jacket. "Henry Rackmeyer, you tell us what is important." "A shaft of sunlight at the end of a dark afternoon, a note in music, and the way the back of a baby's neck smells if its mother keeps it tidy," answered Henry. "Correct," said Stuart. "Those are the important things..."
>
> E.B. White
> *Stuart Little*

Rewards

Everyone needs to feel that what they are doing is valuable. In our century, art has become the lost goal for many. A few years ago a study was conducted on the feelings of elementary school children. They found that in general children enjoy art more than any other single subject, but, at the same time, feel that art is unimportant! Somehow, we are developing an early attitude that insists that we must aim at a different target than "heart" which may explain the continued decline of college majors in music, English literature, and other humanistic disciplines. In their place the monolith of business has become the attraction that is the

Holy Grail of our time. People rarely think of attending college for an education (i.e., learning to think); they are there as a way station for a job.

Often those in church choirs are the minority who feel that deeper is better. Many, somehow, have escaped, at least temporarily, from the quagmire of the illusive money trail and realize that singing church music enriches their lives and those around them. They devote sixty to ninety minutes a week to attend a practice, so that the Sunday worship can hold more meaning for them, as well as the congregation. It is a very personal reward. Those of us who find beauty and true satisfaction in what we do, take from those experiences something impossible to explain to those who shun it. Directors must take a few minutes to remind choir members of that.

The "verbal pat on the back" is common. Saying thanks is important to congealing the group into a unified choir. But, the directors who go beyond surface thanks are the ones whose choir members bring (and take) the most from these experiences. Finding that balance between treating them as a professional group and, at the same time, establishing a posture that this is THEIR church and choir, is not something usually attempted. Directors tend to go in one of those directions, but not necessarily both.

The choir director who moves the singers to a constant series of epiphanies, illuminations, and peak experiences, may not need to explain those rewards; however, reinforcing those times when the choir's involvement was deeper will help the singers realize that there is a difference. Once that occurs, then working toward achieving that level of accomplishment more frequently will follow. Take time to help them grasp that what they are doing is important, and that a personal reward is attained with each new anthem, each release of emotion, and each tiny compliment to another choir member.

Too often, we speak to the choir only in terms of the musical performance (external reward), and while that is valuable, church choirs need the feeling of the ordinary as well (internal reward). Jack Kerouac, one of mysterious heroes of my generation, referred to turning ordinary moments into our destiny as "sacred dust." Just as the E.B. White quote at top of this chapter reminds us that what is important may be the least obvious, the director who ritualizes experiences through a story or an imagined vision, will find that not only will the music become more sensitive, but so will those in the choir. Walt Whitman was not religious in the formal sense of the church, but he did have a philosophy that embraces the church. He said, "I believe, that a leaf of grass, is no less than the journey work of the stars. The smallest sprout shows there is really no death."

Rewards that are more obvious also are found within the church choir. These kinds of rewards are understood more easily than those philosophical ones mentioned above. Try to give your choir both types.

Service Recognition

In the past, Sunday schools gave circular pins and additional bars to those with perfect attendance. Most of the children/youth did not wear them to church, but still had a sense of accomplishment by receiving them. Church choirs should not focus on weekly attendance, but rather on yearly involvement. Purchasing and distributing pins or certificates for members is an inexpensive, yet permanent remembrance. Start by distributing a certificate for service of one year. More attractive pins of greater value could be distributed to those having five years of service to the church choir. This five-year increment could continue for those with ten, fifteen, and twenty years of service. See Chapter Nine, Resources: Part Two for suggested materials.

Those with ten or more years of service should be recognized to the congregation. In addition to the "in-house" distribution of the pins, place their names in the bulletin. For those with twenty years of service, there could even be a short ceremony in which the minister presents the pin and/or certificate. Even though directors may feel that this approach is not needed, the clear majority of the choir will appreciate the fact that what they are doing has recognized value.

End of the Year Recognition

The simplest form of recognition, which should be done each year, is to identify the names of every person who sang in the choir that year by placing them in the bulletin on the choir's final Sunday before the summer break. Those choirs who function the full twelve months will need to find the appropriate time for this goodwill gesture.

Repeated Repertoire

Another modest way of showing appreciation is to have the choir vote on their favorite music sung during the year. Those pieces then could be used (if liturgically appropriate) within the service during those weeks of May when membership starts to sag. These choices also could be the basis for music sung during the summer when the choir might gather for a quick pre-service rehearsal and performance to rejuvenate the summer services. Identifying the music that the choir most enjoyed will also be a help in selecting future repertoire. Certain styles and moods that have special appeal to the singers should be a part of those new anthems selected for the coming year.

Composing/Arranging for the Choir

For those conductors who have the skill to arrange and/or compose, creating a new work for the choir to "premiere" is a personal method of saying thanks. Be sure to place a dedication to the choir at the top of music, and to include this dedication in the bulletin when the music is first performed.

Frequently, there are choir members who have compositional ability; using their music throughout the year is a special recognition that is highly recommended. This music need not be a complete anthem; music could be created by choir members which could serve as incidental music for introits and prayer responses. Many members may not have the ability to write an extended composition, but there will be those who could write brief, undeveloped phrases of music for incidental use. Singing their original music, even though it may not be of exceptional quality, will make a bold statement to the choir.

Commissioning

Commissioning new music has been discussed earlier, but directors should be reminded that this is an excellent opportunity to recognize people. To commission a new work to celebrate a member's extended service to the choir combines several valuable elements. This also could be done for the organist who has labored for many years. A new organ work or an anthem which has a featured organ solo is a musical way to show appreciation.

Choir Picture

Although it is possible to have a formal picture taken of the choir, an unannounced picture taken during a service or at some other time when the choir is in their robes is very useful. Have the picture duplicated so that each choir member receives one (even those who were not there for the picture). They could be given as a Christmas card or gift to each person.

Another highly useful aspect of pictures is to have one taken early in the fall and made into a large photo for the wall. Place the names of everyone either on the picture, or in such as way that people will be able to learn the names of the choir. Surprisingly, not everyone in large choirs truly remembers the names of people who may have been in the choir for years.

Take pictures of new choir members and place them on the bulletin board within the choir room. This is a warm welcome to them and will help old members learn the names of new personnel.

Socializing

Several times throughout the year take it upon yourself to bring refreshments for after the rehearsal. These occasions should not be announced ahead of time and should be a happy surprise. Stop the rehearsal early so that everyone can stay and socialize. To merely bring refreshments and have them at the end of a long rehearsal will not be effective. Many people have set schedules, so to stay longer for a social time is not possible. By ending the rehearsal fifteen minutes early and calling this to the choir's attention, the director makes a far different statement of purpose, and truly encourages them to be interactive with each other.

Time Off

Not all churches will have the possibility of allowing the choir to skip a Sunday. Ministers want the choir there to assist with the hymn singing and add depth to the service. Yet, there are times of the year when giving the choir a Sunday of no responsibility is recommended. The weeks after Christmas and/or Easter are periods following intensive musical contributions from the choir. These are ideal times to have a soloist or visiting group provide the music for worship services. Choir members may sit with their families, attend a different service within the church, or, more commonly, miss a Sunday without guilt. These "breathers" are needed. A weekly commitment is easier to fulfill when there are times that provide relief. Building these times into a regular schedule will be appreciated by the members; to have them following a period of high involvement from the choir also encourages them to adjust their schedule for the extra rehearsal or performances associated with that period (i.e., Holy Week).

Find ways of rewarding your choir and showing that they are appreciated. Even though St. Ignatius Loyola in the fifteenth century said, "Teach us, good Lord, to serve Thee as Thou deservest...To labor and not ask for any reward save that of knowing that we do Thy will," the wise director will disregard that admonition and find ways of affirmation and reward for every single person in the choir.

CHAPTER 11

> The Church knew what the Psalmist knew: Music praises God. Music is well or better able to praise Him than the building of the church and all its decoration; it is the Church's greatest ornament.
>
> Igor Stravinsky
> *Conversations with Stravinsky*

Reminders

Some wag once said that "Responsibility simply means the ability to respond." Having a reservoir of ideas will not guarantee solutions or success, but not having them certainly increases the risk of failure. Church choir directors are faced with weekly public performances. There is little time for easing a choir into perfection as with auditioned community groups who rehearse several compositions for weeks before singing them on a concert. The old "trial and error" process is not an option in church choirs; their rehearsals must solve problems quickly and result in a prepared, motivated group who will arrive on Sunday morning with the enthusiasm and confidence that they will make a difference. Helping a congregation to understand the Word of God is not a light hearted task!

Previous chapters have provided a compendium of suggestions on specific topics related to church choirs. With each item, several defining and additional recommendations were made to help explain the various points. This chapter, however, is a rapid-fire listing of diverse ideas loosely categorized under two broad areas: THINGS TO DO; THINGS NOT TO DO. In many instances, they are reminders of information that experienced directors already know.

Things to Do

1. Enhance your worship with choir descants for hymns. Purchase and use prepared descants that can be sung on concluding verses of traditional hymns. This adds color to the congregational singing, encourages more vigorous congregational singing, and will help the hymns build to a more emotional climax. (See descant recommendations in Chapter Nine.)

2. Establish a choir roster with names, addresses and telephone numbers and distribute it to the choir. Make additions as new members join.

3. Organize a "telephone tree" for contacting choir members. This tree is structured as an expanding fan so that contacting one person results in their contacting four more people on the list. This simple method saves the director's time and makes it possible to distribute important (immediate) information quickly such as canceled rehearsals, hospitalized choir member, and other similar problems.

4. Review your interpersonal skills so that you:
   a. Learn to listen carefully to someone.
   b. Develop a caring relationship with EACH member.
   c. Learn to manage conflict.

5. Develop a series of creative visual images to give singers. Try to bring one new one to each rehearsal. Some starting suggestions are:
   a. Spin the tone on the breath.

    b. Make that entrance like it's shot from a gun.
    c. Sing to avoid blowing out a candle. (excessive air escaping)
    d. Let the line be more liquid.
    e. Sing through the entire phrase and connect all of the words.
    f. Let your faces be a mirror of the text.
    g. Make the music be more compelling.
    h. That final chord should radiate like the sun.

6. Form a Director's Advisory Committee and meet with them at least twice a year to solicit suggestions for improving any phase of the church's music program.

7. Create and submit a detailed yearly budget that includes items in both Operating Expenses and Capital Expenses. Be specific.

    Example: Chancel Choir Ministry

a.	Sunday anthems (12 new anthems, 50 copies at $1.20 a copy)	$720
b.	Cantatas for Christmas and Easter (50 copies each at $5.50 a copy)	$550
c.	Additional instrumentalists ($50 for rehearsal and performance; 10 needed for orchestra and obbligato lines)	$500
d.	Replacement copies of music due to increased growth of choir	$100
e.	Robe cleaning (50 robes at $6 each)	$300
f.	Tune rehearsal room piano (twice per year)	$130

Do this for each area of your program. Each church will have individual needs; some areas to include might be:
   Children's Choir Ministry
   Youth Choir Ministry
   Handbell Choir Ministry
   Instrumental and Vocal Solo Ministry
   Instrumental Repair (organ, handbells, additional pianos)
   Outside soloists for chapel service
   Leadership training/festivals
   Salaries of Music Staff with "minimum" 3% raise

8. Host touring ensembles who will perform in your church. Church groups, college choirs, and other types of ensembles often will perform in your church in return for lodging and food. Door receipts from the concert might be split between group and church, benefiting both. Be sure to contact other churches and schools in the area as part of the publicity process.

9. On times such as Christmas Eve or Easter, when the choir is performing for several different services, have each choir member bring a refreshment item (juice, cookies, etc.) so that between these events, a social occasion occurs.

10. For early morning services, remind choir members to begin warming up their voices on their way to church (in the car). This will assist them with the untimely hour for singing.

11. At the beginning of each year, assign each singer a secret prayer partner for the coming season. This thoughtful gesture adds strength and depth to your choir. Assign someone to maintain the program to replace departing members and accommodate new singers.

12. Find out additional areas of expertise of choir members.

Reminders

Seek information on interested/competent vocal soloists, on additional instruments people can play, dramatic experience, etc.

13. Put your choral library on a computer program which can be easily updated. Be sure to use cross referencing so that both English and foreign language titles are listed; also file everything by composer/arranger.

14. Remind singers to enter their choir loft in the spirit of the service and not to talk, especially during the organ prelude. They should help establish the mood of the service for the congregation. This is particularly important when the choir loft is in front of the church.

15. Throughout the time the choir is in the sanctuary, before and during the service, all eyes and attention should be focused on what is happening (minister, baptisms, children's sermon, etc.).

16. According to Lewis G. Douglass in *Resolving Church Conflicts* (Harper & Row Pub.), conflict management points are:

   a. Help others feel better about themselves.
   b. Strive for effective communication.
   c. Examine and filter assumptions.
   d. Identify goals, what is wanted.
   e. Focus on primary issues.

17. Spend extra time on diction and remind the choir that their primary function is presenting the Word of God, so clarity of singing is of paramount importance.

18. Establish lines of communication with the congregation which extend beyond merely putting the title/composer in the weekly bulletin. Include anthem texts and brief comments about the music which will help them under-

stand the music in relation to the service, and the scripture of the day. In the monthly all-church newsletter, provide useful information about the music and performers. For churches having multiple services, list who is performing at each service for the month, i.e.,

  Oct. 2, 8:00 am Jack Smith, tenor
      9:30 am handbell choir
      11:00 am chancel choir

19. Provide the church secretary/staff with a recommended list of performers for use at weddings and funerals. Have clearly established guidelines of responsibility for contracting musicians, fees for their services, and information regarding appropriateness of music for each area. Keep this information in a permanent book that remains in the church office.

20. Work closely with the people in charge of providing baby-sitting for the church. Be certain this service is available for regular and additional choir rehearsals.

21. Set personal goals for growth and with each new year increase them. For example a starting list might include the following:

 a. Attend one church music workshop a year.

 b. Purchase and study at least five new types of resources a year (i.e., books, videos).

 c. Introduce one new dimension into the church program each year, i.e., liturgical dance, choir exchange.

 d. Involve different choir members as evaluators who sit apart from the choir during a rehearsal to listen objectively and then give comments to choir and director about diction, balance, etc.; alternate who is selected for these "private concerts" so that all eventually participate.

22. Attend at least one church music workshop a year either with or without financial support from the church.
23. Remember Duke Ellington's admonition: "A problem is a chance to do your best."

Things Not to Do

1. Assume! Check details ahead of time.
2. Start the conducting pattern without bringing hands to a complete halt in a raised in position. Tempo is determined from that position through the anacrusis beat.
3. Permit members to chew gum during rehearsals/services.
4. Permit singers to rehearse without a pencil in their folders.
5. Turn around and bow during a service when the congregation applauds. This suggests that the choir is performing a concert rather than contributing to a worship service.
6. Say at a choir rehearsal:
    a. "It's time to start the rehearsal, but let's wait until more members arrive."
    b. "Let's sing through this new piece to see what it sounds like."
    c. "Ok, that was good. (pause) Let's do it again."
    d. "That was terrible, do it again."
    e. "We need to be better at measure 43, start at the beginning."
    f. "Let's run through _____ (the hymns for Sunday, the anthem in the choir loft, etc.)."
7. Use threats to insure survival.
8. Think of the congregation as an audience (or use that term).
9. Forget that copyright laws apply to churches. See *The*

Church Guide to the Copyright Law (Christian Ministry Resources) by attorney Richard R. Hammar.

10. Evaluate the success of your program based on numbers of people in the choir rather than progress toward clearly defined goals.
11. Forget ethnicity in selecting music or avoid singing in languages other than English in order to capture true flavor of the music.
12. Forget to seek help from others in the choir, the church, and the community.
13. Think of yourself as conductor rather than spiritual leader.

Start with these miscellaneous items and then work backward into the suggestions of the other chapters. Of importance is the recognition that each church program can expand. By taking risks in unchartered territories, church music directors can help make theology stronger, more reflective, and certainly more meaningful to the congregation.

The church staff is a team; if they are all pointed in the same direction of creating substantive worship opportunities, then broad approaches will be required from each person on the team. Often, the only formalized training in "official" church areas will be the minister/priest. Church staffs frequently are comprised of interested lay people who came to their positions from other professional areas of training (i.e., corporate secretary, person with degree in psychology, high school choral director). Even though they bring unique skills to the staff, they must adapt them to the church environment. Those who have been a part of a church system realize that, as with other heterogenous organizations, there are a multitude of daily complications such as conflicts of personality, philosophy, and priority. While striving to be a sanctuary of hope, the church still is comprised of humans, and we all know that their history is filled with combative hostilities.

Bringing new ideas and directions into the church will not always be embraced. The director will need persuasive talents, not only with the musicians, but also with the staff and congregation whose agendas have been predetermined. Yet, without exciting, fresh approaches to the worship service, the church may continue its loss of members. The twenty-first century will, in fact, be a pivotal period in the life of the church. The twentieth century has seen serious attacks on it, with such developments as the "God is Dead" movement, the holocaust, and the neglect of the third world.

David Tame in *The Secret Power of Music* says, "Music may also play a far more important role in determining the character and direction of civilization than most people have until now been willing to believe." From the ancient Chinese, Egyptian, and Greek societies through those of today, music has had a strong influence. Music therapists recognize its healing potential in the same way the church understands its "emotional" energy. Although using a chamber orchestra to accompany a cantata may not seem to have the power of Joshua's Seven Rams' Horns, there is a link. It is impossible to imagine someone who has never had an emotional response (positive or negative) to some type of music. Music touches. St. Augustine knew that when he encouraged its use in the church. His words at the end of the fourth century in his monumental work *Confessions*, are just as true today. He said,

> "How greatly did I weep in thy hymns and canticles, deeply moved by the voices of thy sweet speaking church! The voices flowed into mine ears, and the truth was

poured forth into my heart, whence the agitation of my piety overflowed, and my tears fan over, and blessed was I therein."

As church music directors approach their rehearsal preparations, staff meetings, and worship services, they should remind themselves (and their choirs) of that.

CHAPTER 12

> And, O those voices of children singing under the dome!
>
> Paul Verlaine
> *Parsifal, A Jules Tellier*

Remaining Choirs
Children's Choirs

Happily, in the past twenty years there has been a notable increase in the development of children's choirs. While the thorough blossoming of young singers has been a vital part of music education in England for centuries, America's approach to this has been spotty at best. Many opportunities for children to sing were available, but only recently has a concerted effort been made to propagate "advanced" groups. Singing is work, and only too often children's groups emphasized the lighter side of the process.

Developing good children's choirs requires careful planning, patience, clever motivation, and instantaneous success. Since the attention span of children is limited, there must be shorter attainable goals. When working with young singers with limited background there is so much to teach that the director often feels overwhelmed.

Church size will determine the number of children's choirs possible. There should be no less than two (K-third grade and fourth-sixth). Many primary groups do not include kindergarten children. Common arguments are their highly limited ability versus getting them started in the program. A strong consideration is the size of the group; if the number of older children in the primary group is small, then too many kindergartners will not add musical content, and, in fact, may be a detriment.

The lower level primarily is taught by rote, and usually features cute movements and gestures. Their music is highly repetitive with simple texts, memorable melodies, short phrases, and unison singing.

The upper level choir usually has a more formal approach with specific training in vocal production, diction, and other singing traits. They use music and often perform short cantatas and "light" musicals involving limited costumes/sets, such as Allen Pote's *Oh Jonah!* (Choristers Guild). Often these groups incorporate small instruments (drums, chimebars) into their performances.

Rehearsal times pose problems. Having both groups practice on Sunday morning after Sunday School eliminates having parents make additional weekly trips to the church. Parents with children in both choirs are accommodated if the groups rehearse at the same time. There should be special rooms in the church for each choir, giving them an identity and home.

Performances should include one regular church service so that parents have opportunities to hear them and the children develop an understanding of music's value to worship. One scenario is to have them perform either immediately before the adult service begins or "officially" as the introit. This could happen once a month which gives choirs short term goals. Again, having them both sing on the same service is helpful to parents with younger and older children. Also, as a motivator for church attendance, use the children's choirs on those Sundays when there may be a lower population such as the first Sunday after Easter. Avoid adding them to a service on typically high attendance times such as Christmas Eve or Easter. It is possible to have a separate Christmas Eve service in large churches where multiple services are needed. The children's groups could provide much of the special music for a late afternoon service; this is popular with adults not wanting to wait for evening services on Christmas Eve because of travel and other family obligations. They are a very welcome addition to church concerts and always increase the size of the audience.

Children's choirs are an investment in the future of our choral art and church music in particular. Communities having a children's choir program separate from the schools are fortunate. These ensembles should be encouraged and supported. There are many national associations which provide materials to directors of children's choirs, with the Choristers Guild of Texas as one the largest. Their motto, "the spiritual growth of children and youth through music" is an appropriate axiom for all of us.

> Remember now thy Creator
> the days of thy youth.
>
> *Ecclesiastes, 12:1*

Youth Choirs

As with the elementary age, youth choirs tend to fall into two categories. With larger, active churches it may be possible to have a youth choir for both junior and senior high school levels. Many churches, however, combine these levels into one choir so that a comfortable sized group is maintained. As children age, there are more after school opportunities for them, and unless the church has a highly skilled youth director, involvement of older youth may shrink. There is no set pattern regarding the music leader; the youth music director may be the same person as for the adult choir, or in larger churches, someone different.

Some churches consider the youth choir as pre-high school and permit interested high school singers in the adult choir. This has mixed results and is not recommended in situations where there are as many high school singers as adults.

Youth choirs perform SAB and SATB literature. In churches where they are firmly established and developed, their role in worship services may be significant. As with children's choirs, they may participate as an occasional ancillary group or, in some cases, may be assigned the responsibility for a complete service once a month.

Sometimes, youth groups provide the music for "contemporary" services where a more casual type of music (pop or light rock) is used. Here, special arrangements with less traditional church instruments (electric guitars, drums) dominate. An instrumental ensemble is the accompaniment backbone and replaces the organ which becomes an orchestral augmentation. Music for these groups rapidly has increased in availability. Some starting suggestions for novice directors are:

Exalt Him!. Word Music.
(old and new music with modulations and transitions to assist with medleys)

Standing Order Program. Integrity Music: Hosanna.
(new resource materials sent every four-six weeks includes printed music, cassette for score study, and related items needed for effective services)

Marantha Praise Band. The Benson Company.
(three volumes of choral music with rhythm charts)

Songs of Praise and Worship. Word Music.
(253 selections with diverse orchestrations, percussion and rhythm charts)

Rehearsals often coincide with evening youth activities in the church, particularly Sunday night when there are fewer public school events. Organizing youth choir times depends on the director; when the same person is used for youth and adults, Sunday morning rehearsals will not be possible because of conflicts with regular worship services and pre-service rehearsals.

Securing a director from one of the local high school music programs increases youth interest. Frequently students not normally involved in a church will participate in a youth choir because it is the same music director as they know/respect from their own high school.

Typically, youth choirs will present an annual church musical each year. This may be the connecting link for many of the singers. Costumes, sets, lighting, and other theatrical elements are standard production components. Many churches use tape backgrounds for the music, but this should be discouraged in favor of live music. Tastes will vary according to the director and church. Some publishers who provide a useful starting point for musicals are Integrity Music (1-800-239-7000) and Lillenas Music Creations (1-800-456-4966).

Youth choirs need a unique kind of nurturing; motivating teenagers requires a balanced approach to music and activities. Highly recommended is John Yarrington's recent book, *Building the Youth Choir* (Augsburg Fortress) which is an expansion of his 1980 publication working with this age level. If inspiring leadership is given, youth choirs can be one of the most dynamic forces in any church music program.

> Keeping time, time, time,
> In a sort of Runic rhyme
> To the tintinnabulation that so musically wells,
> From the bells, bells, bells, bells.
>
> Edgar Allen Poe
> *The Bells*

Handbell Choirs

In the past two decades, handbells have become a thriving part of most church music programs. Musically active churches often have several handbell choirs involving children, youth and adults. Although primarily associated with churches, they have become a part of many school classroom experiences as well.

Handbells, while expensive to purchase, have immediate returns. They do not require extensive individual practice to master basic skills. Unlike other musical instruments, they produce a beautiful tone (sound) with the most inexperienced performers. They develop ensemble facility and do not require solo home practice or purchase, as with other instruments. Young ringers can be given just one bell and be an immediate ensemble member in a "gestalt" experience.

Music reading is useful, but for the early stages, it is possible to learn by rote or with less formal reading techniques involving "lines and spaces." Diverse age levels can participate in the same handbell choir, and create engaging music that will mesmerize a congregation. There is a comforting tranquility that emerges with full or reduced choirs (octaves) of handbells.

Listeners enjoy observing a handbell ensemble. They are fascinated as they watch the ringers rapidly put down and pick up different bells or play two bells with one hand. Techniques such as plucking and/or swinging are quickly learned and also provide interesting visual impacts on a congregation.

Vast amounts of handbell literature are being developed. Music for handbells with other instruments, as well as with singing choirs, is readily available. Publishing companies have extensively expanded their catalogues with all kinds of handbell literature. Workshops to assist directors in beginning and advanced teaching techniques are found throughout the United States. In short, a mild revolution quietly has taken place, and handbell skills have become expected for most church musicians.

There are numerous resources for the new director. One that is recommended which provides extensive historical background as well as instruction and music, is *The Liturgical Use of Handbells* (G.I.A. Publications) by Richard Proulx. Other useful sources may be found in Chapter Nine, Resources: Materials.

Remaining Choirs

> The Spirit of the Lord came upon
> Gideon, and he blew a trumpet.
>
> *Judges 6:34*
>
> And the people piped with pipes,
> and rejoiced with great joy, so
> that the earth rent with the
> sound of them.
>
> *I Kings*

Music with Additional Solo Instruments
Flutes and Trumpets

The two most common instruments added to choral singing, especially in church, probably are the flute and the trumpet. They provide very different moods. The flute, quite often is a gentle addition that flows into the music and adds a passive or haunting quality; it blends well with the voices and/or organ. The trumpet tends to be used with a stronger, bravura style. It is majestic or festive, but has the tendency to overpower a choir unless the performer is very sensitive to the situation.

Both instruments have numerous players, and usually can be found in abundance in most congregations. There are many settings and arrangements with choirs. What makes these instruments used so frequently? A survey of any public school band program will reveal that these are popular instruments. Although they are not considerably easier to play than most other band instruments, they are easier than some. Both have ancient Biblical history and use.

The flute, one of man's oldest instruments, dates from primitive times. Its association with religious ideas existed thousands of years before Christ. Early civilizations in Sumeria and Egypt were well-known for their orchestras which included flutes. An early Hebrew musical instrument, the ugah, was a long, wide vertical flute commonly associated with shepherds; it is mentioned four times in the *Bible, Gen. 4:21, Job 21:12, 30:31, and Psalm 150:4*.

Flute lines can cut through the choral texture without dominating it, and especially, without encouraging the singers to oversing. There is a current tendency in choral scores to find that the composer/arranger suggest some kind of C instrument rather than specifically asking for a flute. While the flute functions comfortably as an obbligato instrument, directors are encouraged to choose music in which the flute plays a role that extends beyond that. The flute has a wide range and many lovely indigenous effects that add color to the music; some of these effects include the trill, the flutter-tongue, and tone-bending. Using music with these sounds will broaden the musical depth of the singers.

Trumpets add excitement and have been a part of worship music since the days of the Old Testament. In the New Testament, *Revelation of St. John the Divine*, we hear, "I was in the Spirit on the Lord's day, and heard behind me a great voice, as of a trumpet."

The trumpet's natural sound is strong and penetrating and the problem is that they (all brass) tend to cover the choir. This can be controlled through dynamics, having them play into their stands, and separating them from the choir. For hymn singing their use is recommended to help lead the congregation on the melody or as an obbligato line which soars above them and can be easily heard.

Be reminded that trumpets are pitched in various keys;

the two most common are Bb and C. Directors must be certain that they provide performers with printed music that is in the same key as their instrument. Many problems have developed because the performer only has a Bb trumpet, but is given music that is written in C or vice versa. Also, remember that trombones do not transpose.

Brass quartets using trumpets and trombones have become a standard format for festive music. A quartet of two trumpets and two trombones exactly matches the SATB choir in terms of typical ranges of notes. Furthermore, if C trumpets are available, a brass quartet can then play directly from a hymnal as an accompaniment for congregational singing.

There are many excellent settings of choir/brass music. Easter morning is a common time for including brass; directors are urged to contract the brass players early since most churches will be seeking solid players for those services.

> Let the word be the master of
> the melody, not the slave.
>
> Claudio Monteverdi

Textual Concerns
Gender Issues

Recent societal changes have resulted in a textual gender controversy for the church. Many hymns, for example, only use the male designation (man, him, mankind) and with the current philosophical standards, this bias against women has become a significant issue in many churches. Clearly, nineteenth-century attitudes were such that there was bias, and women were not seen on the same levels as men, so creating hymn texts with this position naturally evolved.

Sorting out the abundant problems in these hymns/anthems eventually will occur. For now, directors and ministers will need to be advocates for the changes through the following suggestions:

1. Avoid purchasing new anthems which do not reflect the gender equality.
2. Develop a systematic approach to adjusting old texts of hymns and anthems already owned by the church. Using "creator" as a substitute is an accepted change; this neutralizes gender, but does not always fit comfortably in terms of syllables to notes or rhyme schemes. If necessary, alternate the use of she/he, her/him, etc. within verses on hymns or for entire hymns.
3. Carefully review all music to be used; plan explanations and substitute words for easy, clear exchanges.
4. Develop a choir/church policy regarding these issues.

Put it firmly in writing and distribute it to the congregation.

Text Value

It is important to choose music with a meaningful text. Members of a congregation often judge the value (and success) of an anthem not by its musical worth or performance, but rather by its text. Most of us would agree that all three factors—musical value, text, and performance—determine its success. Furthermore, we probably would acknowledge that without a fervent message in a fresh musical setting the anthem is, somehow, less. To hear the best and most beautiful words in a banal, trite musical environment is, to me, worse than to hear less intoxicating words enhanced by a dramatic effective musical arrangement.

Familiar Texts

Several times a year give the congregation works that have familiar text. They have come to know and love these words. If we include music new to the choir, but based on words that are familiar, we are giving new perspective to the text.

Messages of Hope

It could be argued that a majority of people attend church because of hope. Everyone wants to believe that the future will be better than the past. Immediately following the next silent prayer time, reflect on your thoughts. Were most of the items in your prayer seeking something (hoping) or acknowledging (thanking)? In *The Desert in the City*, Carlo Caretto points out that "Optimism means faith in men (people), in the human potential; hope means faith in God and in the omnipotence," so hope is connected to faith. Include one anthem/offertory a month which features a message of hope.

Textual Groups

As an educational tool, organize music around texts. Psalms, Old or New Testament texts, themes such as Christ's words, will have a more potent influence when grouped into common connections. In *Sacred Texts of the World, A Universal Anthology,* the texts of various religions such as Christianity, Hinduism, Buddhism, Jainism, Taoism, and Confucianism, have been collected. Similarities between texts abound, and certain universal characteristics can be traced throughout the world and down through the centuries.

Choir directors should compile their own useful list of texts found in their church's musical library. With the computer it is simple to create a listing of the texts. They could be organized by books of the Bible, topics, or authors. Organize music choices which connect these texts into three- or four-week units that can bring a new dimension of comprehension to the choir and congregation.

Foreign Texts

The use of non-English texts has been discussed earlier. Standard Latin texts such as *Agnus Dei, Magnificat, Ave Verum Corpus,* should be used occasionally. These church traditions should not be abandoned completely. Always put the translation in the bulletin/program and inform people that the beauty of church Latin enhances the quality of the music.

> Some to church repair
> not for the doctrine,
> but the music there.
>
> Alexander Pope

Coda

A coda usually pertains to music found at the end, but in this context refers to several items that possibly could have been covered in earlier chapters. These miscellaneous thoughts may be of use to some directors.

What Is Church Music?

There has been confusion defining what constitutes Church Music. For example, in the Baroque Period, instrumental chamber music performed at a concert was called Sonata da Camera; if the same music was played in church it was called Sonata da Chiesa. Music having a text may be clearer in terms of content, but does it become "sacred" just because the text is on a religious topic? Is Jesus Christ, Superstar to be considered as sacred music? Furthermore, there are many exquisite choral settings pertaining to nature and other non-church topics which would seem to be very appropriate for church use.

Does one have to believe in God in order to write church music? Certainly not. Ned Rorem, one of America's finest composers has spoken often about being an atheist, yet he has written some glorious music for the church. He approaches composition from the standpoint of craft. Rorem says, "An artist doesn't 'do' art, he does work. " If the work turns out to be art, that's determined by others after the fact." The same may be said for categorizing music as church music.

Robes

There are many robe styles used by churches. Many may have stoles which have color coding identifying different seasons of the church year. Some are plain white tops and have been the same style for centuries. Each church determines the style appropriate for itself. Robes vary in cost, usually about $85-150, depending on the company (See Chapter Nine, RESOURCES: MATERIALS) and the type of material/style.

Usually, raising funds for new robe purchase is easily accomplished. Asking families of the church to purchase one robe is most effective. A short introductory plea from the choir director to the congregation which explains the need for new robes (i.e., old ones are ten years old and falling apart), the cost of a single robe, and the fact that this is a once in a decade opportunity to show appreciation to the choir for their weekly commitment to the church, probably will be sufficient. People enjoy supporting something as visible as a church choir robe, and for years, each Sunday they can see it being used.

During the summer months, when choirs do not perform on a regular basis, it is suggested that they sing without robes. They may sing once a month in the summer, and seeing them in regular clothes instead of robes, gives everyone a nice change. Then, in the Fall when the choir officially returns to its weekly duties, the addition of the robes gives the service a more formal spirit.

Robes need to be cleaned at least every other year, and probably should be cleaned after each year of use. Check the church roster to see if any members are in the cleaning business; they may give the church a very special price for robe cleaning.

Hymn Singing

Hymns have been discussed in several chapters, but here are a few additional comments. Generally, hymns are better at a faster rather than a slower pace. If the organist plays them too slowly, they drag and lose their effectiveness. Congregations do not have the breath control of the choir, and a slower pace causes them to breath often and lose the connection of the textual phrases. On those times when additional instruments are available to play the melody, or for hymn festivals a recommended arrangement for singing the various stanzas is:

> Stanza One: all in unison
> Stanza Two: all in parts or women or men alone
> Stanza Three: choir alone in parts, maybe unaccompanied organ interlude (partial or complete stanza)
> Stanza Four: all in unison

Seasonal Bulletin Groupings

To help the congregation see relationships and patterns in services, create multiple-listing bulletins/programs. Advent, for example, is an excellent time to organize all of the Sunday services for the four weeks of that period into one gigantic collection of worship orders. Instruct congregations to return these "booklets" to the pews instead of taking them home as many do.

Each service could focus on one Advent theme with separate subtitles to help with the organization for each week; or, there might be consistent topics used throughout the four weeks. Having them together in one booklet that could be reviewed each week will result in better understanding. This type of service grouping will require very careful advance planning in order to include all hymns or special music for the entire Advent season. Groupings, however, will give the congregation an opportunity to see the linking of past and future services. Separate weekly calendars and announcements can still be distributed by the ushers.

Finally, directors are urged to remain optimistic, enthusiastic, and grateful for those many dedicated musicians who share their time and talents with the church. Remind your singers that they are *making a difference* to the life of the church, and do all you can to help them enjoy their musical contributions. Perhaps the poet George Herbert said it best in The Temple when he commanded,

> Let all the world in ev'ry corner sing,
> My God and King.
> The church and psalms must shout,
> No door can keep them out;
> But above all, the heart
> Must bear the longest part."

Appendix A

Sanctuary Choir
NEWSLETTER

April 5, 1996

Easter Week Memories

I do hope that each of you has received the wonderful comments from the congregation and staff as I have. This may have been our most successful Holy Week ever. From the festive music of Palm Sunday, through the meaningful music of Maundy Thursday and the Good Friday Meditation, you helped the congregation better understand this galvanizing week.

Easter was glorious! The comment that kept coming up was that they "got CHILLS of excitement from the music." You helped the church provide three special services that morning.

Bravo to all of you:

1. thrilling and beautiful singing
2. a good solid choir of between 50-60 each service
3. a real sense of security for all music
4. the best between-service refreshment spread *ever*

Other news

I visited with Mary Capel at the hospital yesterday and she seems to be doing better. It is hoped that she will go home within a week. Keep her in your prayers.

Two of our college singers will be presenting recitals at the university next Friday, April 13, 11:00, in the Concert Hall, Jenny Baker (soprano) and Diane Loper (mezzo-soprano).

It is with considerable regret that I report to you that our wonderful colleagues, Sandra and George Aston will be leaving us later this Spring. They are moving to Illinois. The Astons have been outstanding members of the choir and the church for many years and will be missed by everyone who knew them. We wish them well in their new home, job, and church.

The choir will not rehearse on April 29 and will not sing that following Sunday, May 2. Enjoy your time off. A guest choir from Nebraska Wesleyan will be here to sing that morning.

Our next major work will be a Buxtehude cantata with chamber orchestra that will be sung on Pentecost Sunday, May 22.

Again, thanks for your continued support of this choir and church. You folks really make a significant contribution to the worship services for our congregation.

Appendix B1

FUMC MUSIC SCHEDULE: Fall 1996

	8:00	9:15	10:45
Sept. 8 *Rally Day*	solo	Sanc. Ch. + Brass Quartet	Sanc. Ch. + Brass Quartet
Sept. 15	solo	solo	Sanc. Ch.
Sept. 22	solo	Sanc. Ch. + Children's ch.	Sanc. Ch. + Children's Ch.
Sept. 29	Chamber Ch.	Carillons	Carillons
Oct. 6 *World Communion*	solo	Sanc. Ch. + Orchestra (Mendelssohn Cantata ,20 min.	Sanc. Ch. + Orchestra (Mendelssohn Cantata, 20 min.)
Oct. 13	solo	solo	Sanc. Ch.
Oct. 20	Chamber Ch.	Carillons	Carillons
Oct. 27 *Reformation*	solo	Sanc. Ch. + Orchestra (Bach Cantata 17 min)	Sanc. Ch. + Orchestra (Bach Cantata 17 min)
Nov. 3 *Finance Sun.*	solo	Sanc. Ch + Child. Ch.	Sanc. Ch. + Child. Ch.
Nov. 10 *Stewardship Sun.*	solo	solo	Sanc. Ch.
Nov. 17 *Bible Sun.*	Chamber Ch.	Carillons	Carillons
Nov. 24 *Thanksgiving Sun.*	solo	Sanc. Ch.	Sanc. Ch.
Dec. 1 *Advent*	solo	Sanc. Ch.	Sanc. Ch.
Dec. 8	solo	solo	Sanc. Ch.
Dec.15	solo	Sanc. Ch. + Child. Ch. + Orchestra	Sanc. Ch. + Child. Ch. + Orchestra
Dec. 22	Chamber Ch.	Carillon	Carillon
Dec. 29	solo (harp?)	solo	solo

Church Choir Director's Guide to Success

Special Services

Nov. 27,   7:00 pm   Sanctuary Choir
Thanksgiving Eve

Dec. 24,   4:00 pm   Children's Choirs + vocal soloists
Christmas Eve   6:00 pm   Sanctuary Choir + Carillons + Brass Choir
                      7:30 pm   Sanctuary Choir + Carillons + Brass Choir

Music of the Church Series

Oct. 13,   7i30 pm   The Longstreet Chorale
Oct, 15   7:30 pm   University Chorus/Camerata Singers
Nov. ? (TBA)   Organ Concert
Dec. 8   2:00 pm   Christmas Concert

Advent Mini-Concerts

Dec. 8   9:00 + 10:30   FUMC Chamber Choir
Dec. 15   9:00 + 10:30   Children's Choirs
Dec. 22   9:00 + 10:30   The Carillons

Appendix B2

SANCTUARY CHOIR REPERTOIRE
Fall 1996

Sept. 8 Brass Quartet	8:00	Guest soloist	
	9:15/10:45	Int: Anth: Offer: P. Res: Hymn: Bene:	Pote, FESTIVE PRAISE Courtney, PRAISE THE LORD WHO R. Leaf, ANCIENT OF DAYS Baker, AMEN (#903) Pelz, O GOD OUR HELP IN AGES PAST Schalk, SENT FORTH
Sept. 15	8:00	George Smith, Tenor	
	9:15	Betty Jones, Mezzo-Soprano	
	10:45	Int: Anth: Offer: P. Res: Bene:	Lewis, WE COME TO WORSHIP GOD Parker, THE ANOINTING Hayes, GOD OUR CREATOR Crotch, O COME AND DWELL (#388) Lewis, TO DO THE WORK OF GOD
Sept. 22 With Trumpet	8:00	Carol Waller, Soprano	
	9:15/10:45	Int: Anth: Offer: P. Res: Bene:	Children's choirs Hayes, GUIDE ME O THOU GREAT Martin, BLOW OUT THE TRUMPET Traditional, AMAZING GRACE (#378) Sicilian M., LORD, DISMISS (#671)
Sept. 29	8:00	Chamber Choir Hassler, CANTATE DOMINO Ray, HE NEVER FAILED ME YET	
	9:15/10:45	The Carillons	
Oct. 6 With Orch.	8:00	Guest Soloist (TBA)	
	9:15/10:45	Int: Anth: Off: P. Res: Bene:	Larson, COME SHARE THIS FEAST Mendelssohn, IF YOU RELY Beck, OFFERTORY Berthier, KYRIE ELEISON none

Appendix C

A Good Friday Meditation

PRELUDE
O Sacred Head Now Wounded — Johann Pachelbel (1683-1706)
Jack Wright, Organ

INTROIT
Victimae Paschali Laudes — Tomas Luis Victoria (c.1510-1611)
The Sanctuary Choir

FIRST MEDITATION
Joan Brooks, Reader
Tenebrae Factae Sunt — Michael Haydn (1737-1806)
Ave Verum Corpus — Wolfgang Mozart (1756-1791)
The Sanctuary Choir

SECOND MEDITATION
Christine Murray, Reader
Amazing Grace — American Folk Tune, arr. Jeremy Green
Lamb of God — arr. James Bolen
The Carillon Handbell Choir

THIRD MEDITATION
Anne Winger, Reader
Stabat Mater — Franz Schubert (1797-1828)
The Sanctuary Choir

Were You There (#288) — American Spiritual
The Sanctuary Choir and Congregation

THE HOMILY
Rev. Thomas Meeker

FINAL MEDITATION
Jane Murray Williams, Reader
Lord, Hear My Prayer — James McCray

O Sacred Head Now Wounded — Robert Leaf
The Sanctuary Choir
Mary Putney, Clarinet

When I Survey the Wondrous Cross (#298) — Lowell Mason
The Sanctuary Choir and Congregation

A SELECTIVE BIBLIOGRAPHY

Doug Adams, DANCING CHRISTMAS CAROLS,
   San Jose: Resource Publications, 1978.

Denis Arnold, "Concertato" in THE NEW GROVES DICTIONARY OF MUSIC AND MUSICIANS, VOL. IV, New York: Macmillan Publishers, 1980.

George Appleton, ed., THE OXFORD BOOK OF PRAYER,
   Oxford University Press, 1985).

William J. Bullock, BACH CANTATAS REQUIRING LIMITED RESOURCES
   Lanham: University Press of America, 1984.

Robert Craft and Igor Stravinsky, CONVERSATIONS WITH IGOR STRAVINSKY,
   London: Faber and Faber, 1959.

Richard A Hammar, THE CHURCH GUIDE TO COPYRIGHT LAW,
   Nashville: Christian Ministry Resources, 1981.

Harold Decker and Julius Herford, CHORAL CONDUCTING, A SYMPOSIUM,
   New York: Meredith of Appleton-Century-Crofts, 1973.

Louis Douglas, RESOLVING CHURCH CONFLICTS,
   New York: Harper and Row, 1986.

Winfred Douglas, CHURCH MUSIC IN HISTORY AND PRACTICE,
   New York: Charles Scribner's Sons, 1962.

Quentin Faulkner, CHOIR REHEARSAL PRAYERS,
   St. Louis: Morning Star Music Publishers, 1990.

David B. Guralnik and Joseph Friend, editors, WEBSTER'S NEW WORLD DICTIONARY,
   New York: The World Publishing Co., 1957.

Bibliography

Donald P. Hustad, JUBILATE! CHURCH MUSIC IN THE
   EVANGELICAL TRADITION,
   Carol Stream: Hope Publishing Co., 1981.

Donald P. Hustad, JUBILATE II, CHURCH MUSIC IN WORSHIP
   AND RENEWAL,
   Carol Stream: Hope Publishing Co., 1993.

Cheslyn Jones, Geoffrey Wainwright, Edward Yanold SJ, and Paul
   Bradshaw, editors, THE STUDY OF LITURGY,
   New York: Oxford University Press, 1992.

Hugh Keyte and Andrew Parrott, THE SHORTER NEW OXFORD
   BOOK OF CAROLS,
   Oxford: Oxford Univesity Press, 1993.

Robin Leaver and James Litton, editors, DUTY AND DELIGHT:
   ROUTLEY REMEMBERED,
   Carol Stream: Hope Publishing Co., 1985.

Austin Lovelace, THE ORGANIST AND HYMN PLAYING
   Carol Stream: Hope Publishing Co., 1981.

James McCray and Lee Kjelson, THE CONDUCTOR'S MANUAL
   OF CHORAL LITERATURE,
   New York: Belwin Mills/Warner, 1972.

James Ode, BRASS INSTRUMENTS IN CHURCH SERVICES,
   Minneapolis: Augsburg Fortress, 1970.

Margaret Pepper, editor, THE HARPER RELIGIOUS AND
   INSPIRATIONAL QUOTATION COMPANION,
   New York: Harper and Row, 1989.

Paul K. Peterson, THE SECOND VOICE, DEVOTIONS FOR
   CHURCH MUSICIANS,
   St. Louis: Morning Star Music Publications, 1994.

Richard Proulx, TINTINABULUM: THE LITURGICAL USE OF
   HANDBELLS
   Chicago: G.I.A. Publications, 1980.

Johannes Riedel, THE LUTHERAN CHORALE, ITS BASIC TRADITIONS,
    Minneapolis: Augsburg Fortress, 1967.

Ray Robinson and ALlen Winold, THE CHORAL EXPERIENCE,
Prospect Heights: Waveland Press, Inc., 1976.

Erik Routley, THE MUSIC OF CHRISTIAN HYMNS,
    Chicago: G.I.A. Publications, 1981.

Erik Routley, THE DIVINE FORMULA,
    Princeton: Prestige Publications, 1986.

Erik Routly, WORDS, MUSIC, AND THE CHURCH,
    Nashville: Abingdon Press, 1968.

Nat Shapiro, AN ENCYCLOPEDIA OF QUOTATIONS ABOUT MUSIC,
New York: Da Capo of Doubleday Inc., 1985.

Carl Schalk, KEY WORDS IN CHURCH MUSIC, VOL. I and II,
    St. Louis: Concordia Publishing House, 1978.

Albert Schweitzer, J.S. BACH, VOL. I and II,
    Boston: Bruce Humphries Publishers, 1972.

James R. Syndor, HYMNS AND THEIR USES,
    Carol Stream: Agape of Hope Publishing, 1982.

Elwyn Wienandt, CHORAL MUSIC OF THE CHURCH New York:
The Free Press of Macmillan Company, 1965.

John Yarrington, BUILDING THE YOUTH CHOIR,
    Minneapolis: Augsburg Fortress, 1996.

INDEX

Advent 60-61
Altos 40
All Soul's Day 68
Anerio 91
Announcement ideas 6
Anthems 80-82
   Memorial anthems 103-104
   Preparation 30-31
Antiphonal music 85
Artistic symbolism 26
Ave Verum 92
Bach's Cantatas 86
Basses 40
Benedictus Domine Deus Israel 95
Books, reference 112-114
Budget 129
Cage, John quote 69
Cantata 85-87
Canticle 85
Carol 83-84
Caroling 52
Children's choirs 137-139
Choir
   All men or women 5
   Choir exchange 18
   Choir newsletter 14
   Dedication Sunday 21-23
   Picture 123
Choral Conducting, A Symposium 38
Choral tone 38-40
Christ the King Sunday 68
Christmastide 61-62
Church Festivals: see festivals
Church survey 7
Church staff participation 24
Collections of music 116
Commissioning
   a choral work 53-56, 123
Computer 1174-118
Concerts
   Benefit 105-107
   Church music survey 97
   Concert/service themes 97-99
Concertato 85, 96
Concerts: mini-advent 44
Contemporary services 49
"Dissolving of I" Ceremony 48-49
Easter 66-67
Epiphany 62-63
Fauré *Requiem* 20

Festivals
   International travel 21
   With another church 20
Frozen tapestry 52
Funding 99-108
Good Friday 20
Gradual 84-85
Guest conductors/composers 26
Hallelujah Chorus 60
Handbell choirs 143-144
Handel quote 98
Herbert, George quote 154
Historian 27
Hymn singing 153
Instruments, music with 145-147
Internet 117-118
Intervals, problem 36-37
Intonation problems 35-36
Last Supper, The 45
Lent 63-64
Liszt, Franz quote 29
Liturgical drama 51
Liturgy 17
Logo for choir 53
Loyola, St. Ignatius quote 125
Magnificat 89-91
Mardi Gras 56-57
Mass 87-89
   Missa Brevis 87
   Solemn Mass 87
Memorial anthems: see anthems
Men's choir 51
Milton, John quote 1
Monteverdi, Claudio quote 148
Motet 82
Music department brochure 3
Music bulletin board 5, 14
Names of members 13
Nash, Ogden quote 99
Networking
   Outside the church 6
   Within the church 4
New person ceremony 10
Newman, Ernest quote 77
Oratorio 94-95
Orchestra 104-105
Organizations 109-111
Oxford Book of Carols 84
Palestrina 91
Palm Sunday 56

164

Church Choir Director's Guide to Success

Passion 65, 93-94
Passiontide 64-66
Pentecost 67-69
Periodicals 111-112
Personal achivements of members 14
Poe, Edgar Allen quote 143
Pop music 140
Pope, Alexander quote 141
Pope Leo XIII quote 108
Post cards 116
Posture/appearance of singers 37
Prayer opeining/closing 31
Processionals: see spacial singing
Rally Sunday 22
Recording, all-church 25
Recruiting 1-10
Recruitment officer/committee 2
Rehearsals 29-45
   Attitude 40, 44-45
   Outline 31
   Elements 66
   Energizing 34
   Oversights 43
   Structure 32
   Tips 41-43
   Techniques 34-35, 43-44
Rejuvenation 47-58
Reminders 127-136
Repertoire 18, 59-98
   Church year 59-69
   Genres 59-69
   Nine month outline 74
   Variety 71-75
Requiem Mass 92-93
Retaining choir members 13-28
Rewards 119-125
   End of year 122
   Repertoire 122
   Service recognition 121-122
Robes 152
Routley, Erik quote 11, 81
Salaries 101-103
Scheduling 16
Section leaders 102-103
Seven Last Words 78-79
Shakespeare quote 10
Shaw, Robert quote 41
Singing faults 37-38
   Audible problems of singers 37-38
   Visible problems of singers 37
Singing styles 34-35
   Spacial singing 18
   Small ensembles (sub-groups) 24-25
Sopranos 40

St. Augustine quote 135-136
Stabat Mater 92
Stravinsky, Igor quote 127
Summer music camp 53
Support ceremony 49
Swan, Howard quote 38
Syrus, Pubilius quote 28
Tame, David quote 135
Te Deum 91-92
Tenors 40
Text
   Familiar texts 149
   Foreign 150
   Gender issues 148-149
   Messages of hope 149
   Value 149
Thurber, James quote 47
Trinity Sunday 67-69
Verlaine, Paul quote 137
Video compilation 8
Videos 114-115
Welcome wagon 9
White, E.B. Quote 119
Whitsunday 67-69
Women's choir 51
Youth choirs 140-142

About the author

Dr. James McCray (b. 1938) is a Professor of Music at Colorado State University and the Director of Music at the First United Methodist Church of Fort Collins, Colorado. He has been a church choir director for over twenty years serving in both Protestant and Catholic Churches. For ten years he was the Chairman of the Music, Theatre, and Dance Department at Colorado State University; prior to that he served as Chair of Music Departments in colleges in Virginia and Indiana.

As a teacher he has received the Professor of the Year Award from the honor societies at two separate universities (Virginia and Florida). In 1992 he received the Arts Award for Creative and Research Activity at Colorado State. In 1997 he was awarded the Mellon Prize for distinguished contributions to scholarship. In 1996 and 1997 he was one of the professors cited for excellent teaching by the CSU Alumni Board.

As a composer he has received numerous commissions from various groups including the Texas ACDA, the Iowa ACDA, the Colorado CSMTA, the Colorado All-State Choir, Central Michigan University, and many more. His music has been performed and recorded by many of today's leading choral conductors.

Dr. McCray's music program at the Methodist Church has more than doubled in the time he has been there. His church choir is recognized as one of the finest in the area; they annually perform more than seventy-five anthems/cantatas for the church. He directs two choirs and supervises a staff who direct the children's choirs, the youth choir, and the handbell choirs.

For twenty years he has contributed a monthly article on church music to the international periodical THE DIAPASON. He has published two other conducting books, twenty-five major periodical articles, over one-hundred music compositions and editions, and in 1998 will publish a two-volume set of books called *American Choral Music in the Twentieth Century*.